PUBLICLY SCHOOLED

One Teacher's Unsettling Discoveries

By Kate Bowers

For my past, present, and future students
And for my colleagues

TABLE OF CONTENTS

THE WOLF AND THE SHEPHERD

A wolf followed a flock of sheep for a long time and did not attempt to injure one of them. The Shepherd at first stood on his guard against him, as against an enemy, and kept a strict watch over his movements. But, when the wolf, day after day, kept in the company of the sheep and did not make the slightest effort to seize them, the Shepherd began to look upon him as a guardian of his flock rather than as a plotter of evil against it; and when occasion called him one day into the city, he left the sheep entirely in his charge. The Wolf, now that he had the opportunity, fell upon the sheep, and destroyed the greater part of the flock. When the Shepherd returned to find his flock destroyed, he exclaimed: "I have been rightly served; why did I trust my sheep to a Wolf?"

-Aesop[1]

CHAPTER 1
SABOTEUR

It felt like an army running at me full speed with swords and spears and anger: "Saboteur! Saboteur!" they vehemently shouted.

I was already overwhelmed. The familiar creep of chronic pain throbbed up my neck and into the back of my skull. No matter what calm reassurances I said to myself or how many prayers I offered up, the pulse of pain remained. At any moment, it could flare up and send me into a dark room, moaning in frustration.

But I had too much to do, students to teach, and boxes to pack. They'd closed my school. The *community's* beloved 166-year-old school. Over and over I felt the anguish and disgust at the decision of the school board.

The staff at my school were scurrying around, snatching up boxes and begging for more packing tape in an odd, heavy-hearted manner. I still had to finalize grades and complete report cards. Wrapped in blankets of sorrow and uncertainty, I'd check in on my colleague's progress. We were all in shock. Eventually we were told where our new school assignments would be; all but two of us were assigned the same school. I began to face the reality of having to say goodbye.

The sad, slow goodbyes to students and parents had melted into a beehive of activity. Yet I found myself at a complete standstill every so often, reliving memories of happy times with students in my classroom. Snapping back to the present, I pressed into completing report cards, packing a box, or cleaning a shelf.

Then the email arrived. *Not now!*

It was a Tuesday morning, the day before the last day of school, when most teachers received the vote-for-contract-ratification email. A list of changes was provided, but an *actual* contract draft was not. Votes were due the next day at 4 p.m. When would I have time to read the changes and make an informed decision? Students would arrive in thirty minutes and be back again the following day. A throb of agony flashed through my already-stressed body.

I prayed unceasingly for strength and wisdom, knowing full well my reply could result in backlash. I took a deep breath and replied-all to the demand to "hurry up and vote!" on a legally binding document we had never seen. Why did we only receive a summary when a draft of the new contract obviously existed? "I would appreciate being able to read the actual contract language and the full contract in order to make an informed vote." To my relief, another teacher also asked for a contract draft; however, a reply separate from the group thread kept us isolated and told the two of us where we could read the *old* contract.

I decided to force the email conversation to happen in the open with a reply-all to every staff member: "Is there a rough draft of the full proposed contract document somewhere?" Yet another teacher responded with the same request. From then on, emails were sent to the entire staff. Teachers were intimidated with the response. "The voting closes today at 4 p.m. As of 8 a.m. this morning, fifty-four [out of 166] people have voted."

We never did get a contract to preview before voting. "[We] do not have contract language to send you . . . If you are unsure about the changes that have been proposed, then please just vote no." Just three hours before the contract vote deadline, a former bargaining team teacher sent an email to all staff: We just had to ratify the contract before summer break, she insisted, or the "contract will stay in status quo, there will be no cost of living increase," and, "I was under the impression that members who do not pay dues do not get to vote. Please check the respondents to make sure those same people are not sabotaging our hard-won gains . . ."

And there it was, my prediction of backlash had come true: I'd been called a saboteur.

CHAPTER 2
BORN TO TEACH

R are was the time when I didn't think I would grow up to be a teacher. A compelling force always pushed me in that direction and I gladly went. Born in the age of disco music and the Watergate scandal, I recall drinking out of the garden hose and learning about the wonder of car seatbelts. Like many children, I let my imagination run wild and taught my stuffed animals, my cousins, and billiard balls how to complete their lessons and line up quietly in a straight line.

After attending a private half-day kindergarten, I entered public school in grade one, then continued through high school in the same district. Graduation couldn't come fast enough, and I raced off to college to get my teaching degree. After substitute teaching for two years in Oregon, I accepted a full-time teaching position in 2001 in Colorado. In 2012, I moved back to Oregon and continued full-time teaching at the elementary level. I completed a master's program in 2015. In the midst of acquiring that degree, multiple questions crossed my mind about the functioning of the public education system in which I was working.

The Common Core standards had flipped curriculum on its head and once-reliable support for discipline issues was now hit-or-miss. A tenet of my faith was to train a child in the way they should go, but policies directed teachers to conform to national standards and step back so children could go where they wished. My beloved teaching profession had warped into something completely unrecognizable.

All too often, people cry "indoctrination" as the easy scapegoat on which to pin the blame for students not receiving a quality education. But what do people really mean when they blame indoctrination? No one names it and certainly no one claims it. It's a vague term thrown out in frustration over a lack of understanding of what's causing public education problems and who is shaping the classroom environment.

The cause of public education woes is sitting right under our noses, the most innocent looking wolf in sheep's clothing. That wolfish shadow on the wall, that figure darting away as soon I glanced over my shoulder, that cold in the pit of my stomach, has been present my entire career—alas—was birthed a few scant years before I was. In the early 1970s, an association began to morph from a collegial support system into an ideological movement determined to take control of the United States of America.

This ideological movement wasn't born here in America. It was imported and personalized with names such as Wundt, Hall, Marx, Mann, and Dewey,[2] purportedly great thinkers, cloaking themselves with altruism and wisdom, preaching from the schools of psychology and uniformity—espousing a public education system that pulls wee babes from their mothers and fathers and tosses them to the care of the government. The shadow of this ideology has steadfastly driven my entire public-school experience. Emboldened by their predecessors' successes, the children of this ideology have dared to step into the light and shatter any wholesomeness public education may have possessed. Now the insidious designer of public education—Mr. Wolfe (that's what I'll call him here, anyway)—is hiding in plain sight.

I've lived through many changes in public education, from Iowa Basic Skills testing as a student in elementary school to the hard task of helping students through the Smarter Balanced Assessment that arrived post Common Core Standards. In my elementary and middle school years, I was unconcerned about the overall structure and powerful force driving public education. Of course it was at work, blindly following the bad advice of Mr. Wolfe, ". . . we are concerned with how to create mass organizations to seize power and give it to the people."[3] I guess he never read our Declaration of Independence or Constitution. In the United States of America, the people *already* hold the power.

Just as I was about to enter my junior year of high school, an economics teacher—about whom I'd heard rave reviews from my brother and cousins—decided to take a sabbatical. I was disappointed I would not get to enjoy his reportedly outstanding class. Instead, the high school guidance counselor taught the class and we ended up filling out tax forms and playing Monopoly™. Not exactly the economics lessons I was hoping for. Is it any wonder me and my classmates were disengaged and demoralized? Didn't anybody care? Mr. Wolfe had so many adherents in public education at that point, I felt the sting of his actions: the loss of a proper education as he inhibited local decision-making, spending, and pursuit of excellent instructors.

As a high school senior, I was required to do a "connections" project. I chose something relevant to my future teaching career and focused on reading instruction. Little did I know I'd stumbled into a hotly debated topic that had been raging for fifty years with Mr. Wolfe influencing from the sidelines.[4] I'm now convinced citizens who can read well are a threat to his desire to control. I dutifully helped a first-grade teacher instruct students in phonics and I passed the project with flying colors, receiving the top score of all seniors for my speech. College courses on teacher preparation would be a breeze, and they were!

As with most teachers, it wasn't until I had my first class as a certified teacher, that I had to grapple with how unprepared I was for the realities of teaching. Student teaching had taught me what *not* to do. It was assumed that because I could read, I knew how to teach reading. It became clear that some college lectures on teaching methodologies were short on actual practice or were misguided.

Roughly twenty years of experience in the classroom have honed my skills. I love investing in students' lives and seeing them grow. I've never stopped pushing myself to learn and improve so that my students can be high-achieving, successful, confident people. Now my push is to improve the awareness of teachers and parents to the lurking powers-that-be making decisions in education today.

Why is it that most people feel *their* child's teacher is phenomenal but simultaneously feel public schools nationally are quite lacking in quality? Who decides what will be taught in schools? Parents? Teachers? Government? Who *should* decide this? It's clear to me, but Mr. Wolfe has his own ideas. How frightening to think I was under his spell for so long doing his sight-word, latest education-trend bidding. No more. I'm joined by thousands of great educators who put their students ahead of their own self-interests and respect parental authority and responsibility. Now, in the midst of a teaching career, hours of research to understand Mr. Wolfe, and the subsequent paper-drenching tears, I share my story about being *publicly schooled.*

CHAPTER 3
OUT-OF-CONTROL BEHAVIOR

Late in 2015, I was frustrated and tense over the out-of-control behaviors present in children at my school. I couldn't pinpoint why they'd worsened. Mr. Wolfe flippantly blamed parents, society, and children's mental health all at once with a trite, "Times have changed."[5] Most students came to school well-behaved and ready to engage in learning. Some were just ornery, which was oddly endearing, but they were manageable. Other students had it rough and brought the weight of their sorrows to school. These burdensome troubles expressed themselves in yelling, tantrums, and running away, to name a few.

I assumed discipline policy still dictated that I manage my classroom in such a way that all students could learn in a secure environment with high behavioral and academic expectations. Nonetheless, under the newest top-down policies, overtly loud and defiant students received only a brief lecture and time playing with playdough before being sent back to class: no real consequences given. Yet an odd sense that I was to blame for poor student behavior hovered in the air like the hot breath of a wolf on my neck.

One day, a young boy gave me a permanent reminder of the hurt some kids carry. Adults, in his young and abused perspective, were the enemy and the cause of his pain. He'd never trust me. Every day he came to class with new strategies designed to elicit a reaction from me. He was not out to get his classmates, but that day he used an attack on them to provoke me. It was his coup d'état.

It had been roughly three weeks since he'd arrived in our room. Oh, how I prayed for him! And myself. And my class. I needed wisdom and help to meet his needs; I couldn't handle the stress on my own. I was given a rundown of his life experiences in a nutshell and my heart was both broken to pieces *for* him and scared *of* him at the same time. I understood why he hated adults; they'd driven him to violence in the past. My muscles had been tense for three weeks. My heart writhed with agony for this little boy who only let me in for one brief moment, days earlier—when he smiled at a joke I cracked. That ear-to-ear, happy smile will stay with me forever because it gave me the briefest glimpse of the boy who could've been.

I was using empty five-gallon paint buckets with lids as reading table stools. During read-aloud I would grab one to sit on, which kept me at a cozy level with the kids sprawled on the carpet, where they enjoyed the day's reading. That day he sat on one too, instead of sitting on the rug with the others. He'd already shown signs of having an "off" day when he threw a few buckets across the empty classroom after the others had gone down to lunch. I had alerted the administration.

I purposely sat in a different spot than usual, a place from which I could better handle any situation. Our desks were arranged in a horseshoe, so everyone in the class was "corralled" on the rug except for him. I began reading, while watching him out of the corner of my eye. His eyes once again conveyed a deeply sinister "I'm going to get you" look.

Of course, I'd been told to document *everything* he did *every single day* in my classroom. Never mind he already had a thick file with a legal document requiring placement in a setting other than the general education classroom. (He'd come from a self-contained classroom, a setting with nearly one-on-one supervision). Never mind he was known to be violent toward adults. Never mind a behavioral specialist had observed and documented him displaying property-damaging, highly disruptive, defiant conduct that should have meant immediate removal for the safety of all involved. Who listened to my concerns? Read my documentation? Was proactive enough to prevent an incident and protect me and my students? My administrative support had sent him back to class. What could I do?

My students had witnessed many days of their new classmate's extreme behaviors. That day, we were all on edge—again. After reading to my students for a few moments, my mind raced in anticipation. What would he do next? It's hard to read aloud and, at the same time, calmly strategize your next move. I saw motion out of the corner of my eye. Surreptitiously, he'd picked up a bucket-stool and raised it over his head. Not once had he hurt the other kids. He was looking at *me*, wanting *me* to react. I froze with fear and indecision. *If I go toward him, he'll throw that at me for sure. He'll believe he's won the "I'm gonna get you" game. My movement may also cause him to throw the bucket at the kids. Better not to react; it's worked before to call his bluff.*

He paused.

I'm trapped.

He looked at the class and released the bucket into the thick of them. Looking back, I realize he gently tossed that bucket, which made sense to me because he was *not* out to get them. He did it to provoke his enemy—me, the only adult in the room.

The round side of the bucket, not an edge, had thumped a classmate in the head. I stood up and firmly told the misbehaving boy to leave the room. I pointed to a chair in the hall, in my fright looking at the chair rather than him. "Go sit in that chair. Your behavior is not acceptable." When I turned back toward him, a bucket was flying at my face. I snapped my hand into the air to deflect it. It caught my hand, spun, and the edge struck my lip and cheek. The class went silent in stunned shock.

He raced out of the classroom. I grabbed my radio and let the office know he was on the run. He hit the principal—who was blocking the front doors—left the school and ran and ran, not even stopping when his shoes came off. The school resource officer picked him up a mile down the busy road.

After I radioed the office, I stepped into the hall to see where he was going. It was then that I touched my lip. The bleeding shocked me and nothing could keep the tears back. Hearing the commotion, a beloved paraprofessional appeared and watched the other students for me. I rushed to the office to check on the boy who'd gotten hit with the other bucket. He had an ice pack on his forehead, but no bump was forming, just a small bruise. He was okay; I was not.

Uncertainty hung in the air as the central district office debated whether to suspend the boy. At the same time, the school resource officer treated me suspiciously and the administration questioned me as if I'd done something wrong. It confirmed my fears that writing office referrals was a waste of my time. Somehow, teachers had become the suspects when kids behaved poorly. Our desire to guide them to more wholesome choices and the achievement of quality characteristics was sidelined every time the central office let students off the hook, which happened more and more often. Naturally, students began to perceive the lax consequences which bred more poor behavior.

I suspected Mr. Wolfe was at the root, working to change the world to what he thought it ought to be—without asking for others' input.[6] A purposeful demoralization of teachers' belief in themselves coupled with destabilization of a school's once-secure learning atmosphere—through discipline policies—was sure to produce a crisis. A crisis Mr. Wolfe would be all too happy to fill with a "new normal" consistent with *his* perception of an ideal education system.

I left school uncharacteristically early that day—at the allowed 3:30 p.m., versus staying one or two hours later. My parents lived nearby and my mom came to the door when I arrived, giving me a big hug while I bawled. They were tears of indignation, not pain. Embers of concern met with sparks of frustration over the treatment of teachers and errant discipline policies. And then roared into angry flames.

CHAPTER 4

TRAUMATIZED AT SCHOOL

The permanent scar left on my lip by the bucket provided a daily reminder that my burning questions about discipline policies needed to be quenched like a desperate thirst. "Their hands are tied," other teachers assured me when it came to the administrative handling of student discipline. By *what?* By *whom?* Why would school leaders go along with anything detrimental to the healthy, productive functioning of their school? I began to dig for answers. I read school board discipline policies. I tracked down state legislation pertaining to student discipline. New legislation had passed, board policies had changed, yet no one had been informed. I didn't know and apparently neither did my fellow teachers. None of it was covered in staff meetings or trainings. I suspected no one informed parents, either. The daily stress of teaching had, along with hours spent searching for answers to school discipline issues, brought on chronic pain flare-ups as relentless as bees in a disturbed hive. Over and over, I asked myself why school districts were not alerting teachers to the policy changes. Wolfe-shaped shadows taunted me, always lurking.

Was I derelict in my duties? Was I expected to read and update myself on board policy changes and new legislation that directly impacted my day-to-day work? Wouldn't school districts consider it a necessary part of ongoing professional development? How else would policies be implemented or effective? I was confused and began to feel like I'd missed a million memos. *Something insidious is afoot,* I told myself for the umpteenth time.

Witnessing my pain, Mom quipped, "I wish you'd stop caring so much!" *She's right,* I thought. If I didn't care about my students, I wouldn't fight for them so hard. I could spare myself a lot of mental, emotional, and physical exhaustion; however, the children's lives would be negatively affected by permissive discipline. I couldn't give up. Mr. Wolfe has convinced thousands, including the teachers he is supposed to protect, that self-interest[7] is a person's sole motivation. I guess I'm proving him wrong.

My parents' faith in Jesus was the model I observed growing up. Through thick and thin, they pointed the family to God, being thankful no matter the circumstances. At times, the circumstances were rough. Not only had the economy tanked in the early '80s, but my dad badly hurt his back and struggled for six months to recover. Our family had to use food stamps. My parents were persistent in their reliance on God and were constantly assured that He would provide. They prayed a lot and Mom would say, "As long as we're all together, we'll be fine. That's what matters." My parents' model of dependence on God planted the seed of faith in my heart.

Fellow churchgoers were encouraging and prayed for our family through what would be called trauma today. I was not permitted to act up at home or school without consequences during this "traumatizing" time. Why were traumatized kids allowed to do so at school?

Withholding healthy, loving discipline from a child is like putting a megaphone to their ear and shouting, "You are not worth the effort. You are not worth the time. You are not loved enough to be given boundaries that are in your best interest." Only Mr. Wolfe would think of such a distressing, detrimental tactic whose only logical result was tumult in schools everywhere and the beginning of the next action/reaction cycle needing attention in America's classrooms.[8]

Recently while I was working part-time as a substitute teacher, I found myself caught in just such a scenario. I was assigned to a fifth-grade class. A girl who hid in her hooded sweatshirt all day got my attention. She drew in her sketchbook, eyes turned down. All day. Coping. Escaping.

Kids ran up and down the halls, hiding in corners, roaming; in their classroom one minute, out the next. Hall passes be damned; no one was checking. Besides, I quickly surmised, the students had discovered that one adult could be played against another. Was the girl's stomach in knots? Did tension pulse in her veins as the noise in the classroom escalated? *What will it be this time? I believe she was constantly wondering. Another room clear? A fight? A screaming match?* Did her head ache with the pounding of yet another slammed door? And what of her nearby classmate, coping only by escaping with her nose in a book?

A few great teachers valiantly pressed on, determined to stay the course amid the lack of expectations and structure. In and out of this girl's classroom came a parade of school staff and administration—unrespected authority figures. None could calm the chaos. With a shock, I concluded that not only was the girl in danger, but so was I.

I, thankfully, was able to leave this heartbreak elementary school and never go back, but the girl in the hooded sweatshirt could not leave. My heart bleeds for the students who—day after day—aren't learning, aren't growing, aren't protected, aren't *seen*. No, their raucous, rebellious classmates get all the attention—and everything they want. Those naughty, in-your-face, outspokenly-defiant kids make my heart ache in a different way than the upright-on-the-outside, cowering-on-the-inside kids. Those cowering silently beg some adult to take control, be in charge, and *protect* them. *Teach* them, maybe?

Other schools I went to had the same loose, frighteningly unsettled atmosphere. I met a teacher whose glasses had been shattered by a student. Another teacher told me about one student shoving another child down the stairs. It was all caught on camera but the perpetrator received no consequences.

Hours of instructional time was being lost to kids undermining the purpose of taking a break. Don't like math? Reading too difficult? Just tell the teacher you need a break. Breaks could be spent in a corner filled with toys. What child *wouldn't* choose toys over the sometimes difficult and messy work of learning? I came to understand that my previous school wasn't an anomaly when it came to lax discipline. Terrible discipline decisions and policies were rampant, exacerbating student trauma.

As a full-time teacher, I frequently commiserated with colleagues across the district about lenient discipline. Usually the chatter blamed the changes in society, economy, and culture. We were brainwashed with messages blaming trauma, poverty, and parents' lack of ability and resources. "Teachers aren't just teachers anymore," district leaders implied. "Kids are unruly because they were traumatized," they said, "and cannot be held to certain behavioral expectations." We were made to believe students were dependent on teachers and schools for *everything*. We walked with shoulders weighed down by the additional roles of counselor, social worker, dad, mom, clothing, and meal provider. These messages of dependency had become ubiquitous, a propaganda from someone on the inside of education, someone with real power to sway an entire nation of approximately 6.1 million public school employees. There was a real but invisible enemy whispering in my ear and grasping me in a chokehold.

Our principals, who were following directives from their superiors (and they, in turn, were following directives passed down from *their* superiors), were one source of the messages that "misbehavior because of trauma should be handled leniently." Why would school district administration say such things? Most, if not all of them, had once been teachers. They understood kids and had children of their own; they should know better. Something didn't add up.

One particular morning, our staff was gathered in a multi-purpose classroom. It was slightly chilly and half the fluorescent lights were off so we could see the projector screen. The tension in the room emanated from the collective stress level of the teachers. Nevertheless, our principal began conveying the talking points she'd been given. We'd heard it before: these kids are traumatized, their parents have no money, their parents are incapable of providing healthy physical, emotional, and mental support, etc.

We were in no mood to hear it so we took control of the meeting, sharing how burdened we felt and how unfair it was to place all the world's troubles on teachers' shoulders. It was mind boggling that we had gotten to a point where room clears, screaming, and door slamming didn't seem out of place anymore. Poorly-behaved students went undisciplined and teachers struggled to handle difficult behaviors on their own. Well-behaved kids who *wanted* to learn were regularly interrupted by out-of-control classmates, creating daily fear and uncertainty—hardly the safe and secure environments we wanted to provide and worked hard to create on a daily basis. We needed support in common-sense discipline and we weren't getting it. On the contrary, students were bribed via point cards to behave well under a program known as Positive Behavior Intervention Support (PBIS), but were not given consequences for misbehavior. "Some kids are being traumatized at home, but now, kids are also being traumatized at school," we told our principal. It fell on deaf ears.

I was mad as a hornet when I became cognizant of the fact I'd begun to believe the "it's poverty, it's trauma, it's the lack of preschool" rhetoric being repeated in my ear. The worst rhetoric was: "it's their parents' fault." We were being programmed to blame the very people who loved the children more than any arbitrary adult inside a school building ever could. Parents are not the enemy; they are the solution. We are going backwards when we believe a *government school* can somehow replace the crucial role of a dad and a mom providing a family unit. The "blame the parents" messengers wanted me to believe abuse, poverty, and trauma are the *rule,* not the exception. And, to believe the schools could solve all of the children's problems. Mr. Wolfe's tactic of school discipline disruption was negatively affecting students, parents, and teachers. The changes he was after were ever-so-stealthily being stacked in place.

The discipline issues at my school were making a once delightful career a stressful morass, causing intense bouts of physical pain. At worst, it felt as though an iron porch rail was being jammed into the back-left side of my head. More than once I crumpled onto my knees and pleaded with God to just make it stop.

It's best to develop a habit of running *to* God in times of trouble, a message I shared with my cabin of campers years ago. It was our evening devotional and I shared with the girls my approach to difficult circumstances, that many people are tempted to become angry with God and turn away from Him in times of distress. The troubles in my school were weighing me down and I knew I needed to heed the very advice I gave those campers years ago. As hard as the issues—and intense rounds of chronic pain—were at school, I needed to lean on my faith. This included being as shrewd as a serpent and as gentle as a dove. I suspected discipline policies were being manipulated by someone even higher up the chain than central district administration. But who? And why?

My angst over issues at school and an inner drive to do right by my students, their parents, and fellow teachers fueled my research efforts to keep digging around for answers. I came across something called the *Dear Colleague Letter,* a product of the Obama administration put out on January 8, 2014.[9] It was there, from the federal level, that discipline policy changes had been dictated. My local school board had changed its discipline policy in February 2014 to follow the new law, it appeared. (Funny, no one bothered to tell the teachers.) In fact, multiple states fell in line without a peep. The federal investigation and litigation that accompanied the *Dear Colleague Letter* were threats school districts couldn't ignore. By 2015, educational assistants helping well-behaved students who were eager to learn were yanked away to babysit the unruly. The invisible chokehold tightened.

CHAPTER 5

TOP-DOWN DISCIPLINE POLICY

Icouldn't wrap my head around it. After reading just four pages of the twenty-three-page *Dear Colleague Letter*, I collapsed under the weight of what I—and my beloved colleagues across the nation—were being accused of: ". . . [S]ignificant and unexplained racial disparities in student discipline give rise to concerns that schools may be engaging in racial discrimination," it said.[10] I couldn't read any further. When I'd recovered a bit, I dug deeper, not willing to accept the accusations directed at all teachers.

I unearthed a 2016 National Education Association (NEA) Policy Statement on Discipline,[11] in which an article by Goldstein and Noguera claimed, "It is the failure of teachers and administrators to acquire cultural competence that leads to the labeling of black youths as out of control and violent. These views lead to punitive disciplinary practices that aim to control students' behavior through security measures in the school, as well as the use of agents of law enforcement and even incarceration." The Statement on Discipline revealed the NEA believes implicit bias exists in teacher discretion, resulting in discipline that is both discriminatory and punitive.

I'm a failure? I lack cultural competence? I punitively discipline my students? My chest hurt, as if an accusatory finger were being repeatedly jammed into it. I'd turned to the teachers union website, falsely believing they wouldn't stand for their teachers being called racists, but instead found that they were one of the loudest accusers. I'm grieved by the fact that racism does exist and is a problem to be eradicated, but accusing every American teacher of it in one fell swoop is an egregious error. A tiny fraction of teachers may be hateful, but I personally don't know any. I'm certain that most teachers in this nation are selfless and loving toward their students.

It's as though the *Dear Colleague Letter* and the NEA discipline statement were grinding away teachers' self-confidence in their ability to assess their own students and handle student discipline. Were school district administrations taking orders from NEA? From the Feds? The shadows looked eerily similar to those of Mr. Wolfe.

I'd always felt the discretion of the teacher, in partnership with the child's parent, is what's best for the child. It's my choice to follow Jesus and the precepts in His Word that enable me to love and respect students even when it's hard. It's that same guidance which rings in my ears: "My brothers and sisters, believers in our glorious Lord Jesus Christ must not show favoritism."[12] And also, "Love is patient . . ."[13] Even though I've been hit, yelled at, chewed out, called names, and more, I love *all* of my students. I want what is best for them and at times have stained my pillow with tears over them.

The relationships I had formed with students over the years were the critical bond that led to student growth in character and academics. One year, I squeezed out several minutes a day to sit next to Kristin, one of my second graders. She would avoid any academic task with every trick she could possibly dream up. After receiving extra attention, and some much-needed confidence boosting, she began to do her work. I promised I would be there to help her.

A few years later, right after lunch, Sam looked at me with a twinkle in his eye and grinned. I couldn't see his teeth, just a bright strip of orange peel. I laughed, which made him laugh, and the peel dropped out of his mouth. The next time orange slices were served at lunch, three or four second graders came to class with orange peel grins. The students were rolling with laughter the day *I* showed up after lunch with an orange peel smile. Our snack on the last day of school was orange slices and we all smiled for an orange-peel picture.

Some relationships were exceedingly difficult or never took root. A particularly incorrigible second grader refused to obey and respect adults. A persistently chatty fourth grader despised my requests for silence. At times, there would be students in my room with whom I never could click. We respected one another and the school year went smoothly, but just as interactions with any group of people, I didn't feel close to all of them. It's those rare times I had to press on and make a conscious, consistent effort to build a relationship anyway.

Have I ever yelled at a student? Guilty. A whole class? Guilty. Made sarcastic statements? Guilty. Said the wrong thing which hurt a child? Guilty. Am I proud of any of those mistakes? *Of course not.* I understood how important it was to admit my mistakes to the individual student, or the class as it were, and ask for forgiveness. God bless them, they always forgave me. It served to strengthen our relationship.

Students under my care come to know when discipline is necessary that no matter what, I would love and respect them. "Love you too much to let you misbehave," I say to remind them how important they are to me.

One year, my group of fourth graders were getting growly and irascible over their assignments and schoolwork. Usually, they were a wonderful, hardworking group, but they'd become slack in their efforts. It was time for a heart-to-heart. I pulled my tall stool up to the front and let out a big sigh.

"I'm going to tell you a story about when I was a little girl," I said. "My mom was making me do chores, like taking out the garbage and cleaning the toilet. I didn't like doing it, and I didn't want to do it, so, I didn't. Well, she gave me a spanking!"

My fourth graders eyes went wide.

"Another time, she'd told me over and over not to do something (I don't remember what it was). I did it anyway. Well, she gave me another spanking!"

The fourth graders looked at one another in amazement, chuckling nervously. "Now, fourth graders, you don't like it when I make you do your work, when you have to miss recess to finish, or when you have a timeout because you were unkind. Why do you think I discipline you? Why do you think my mom disciplined me? She knew that someday I would have important responsibilities I'd have to take care of even when I didn't feel like it. She knew there were dangers in the world and if I didn't learn self-control, I would get hurt. She cared enough to guide me on paths that were in my best interest. She loved me."

Student infractions always culminated in a talk between me and the offending student. I would assure them that nothing they could do would possibly make me stop caring for them. Whether the infractions were big or small, whichever student it was, I reminded them I cared with a gentle fist bump, pat on the shoulder, or "you are important to me" when it was all settled. Just as I'd received a huge hug and an "I love you" after the sting of discipline from my parents, I wanted to reassure my students I cared for them after the sting of loving disciplinary action. How could that kind of discipline and support lead to incarceration or support racism?

Yet, the NEA Policy Statement on Discipline, section B, part 1 is labeled: "Educators' Actions Feed the School-to-Prison Pipeline." The day I read this, my eyes watered, I folded my arms on my desk, and put my head down. All the stress, confusion, and weight of suspicions my administration, school district, and state and federal departments of education had put on my shoulders regarding student discipline burst inside me. Covertly, I *had* been treated as though I were a discriminatory, punitive, whip-lashing teacher. Policies and people *were* judging and finding me guilty of disciplinary crimes I'd never committed. My lip was scarred, my health impacted, and my self-efficacy as a teacher tanked. The intense pressure and expectation to fall in line with the demands of policies I felt were doing harm to kids was just too much.

I imagined Mr. Wolfe chuckling derisively along with some friends at the NEA, merely asking of his discipline-disrupting tactic, "Will it work?"[14] I tried to shake the image out of my head. I could be hurt, steam rolled, and tossed aside. They didn't care.

I felt blindsided by the policy changes, and the discontent amongst my colleagues led me to believe they felt this way, too. Why was the organizational voice of educators allowing school environments where teachers were being treated like incompetent, biased classroom managers?

I kept all my angst over the circumstances bottled up. I was between a rock and a hard place. If my administrators were going along with questionable discipline policies, who was I to speak out against them? Teachers have become accustomed to just taking what's given and applying it in our classrooms. We are warmed to ideas (most likely designed in Mr. Wolfe's office) like a frog in a pot and told to accept them because they came from "expert research" or the latest "improvement" and "many other districts are adopting this new program, curriculum, procedure, or policy." Why couldn't teachers be more like the Jolly Green Giant™, tall and unflinching, when someone offered us tooth-rotting goodies instead of wholesome vegetables?

Now that I knew the origins and content of the policies, I reasoned with a crinkled brow, *I had a responsibility to confront the issue.* If I took the lead and stood tall against absurd policies, could I trust God to be there for me? Surely my unchanging God would show up to improve the plight of students and teachers locked into imposed, ineffective discipline policies, just as He'd shown up to care for me in other situations throughout my life.

How could I withstand the increased pain and stress that would come with advocating for better discipline policies than those implemented by the *Dear Colleague Letter?* I was learning to live with the possibility of pain striking any day at any moment. Added stressors made things worse. I could accomplish so much more for students if I were just *free* of this near constant ache. I believed God's strength is made perfect in weakness.[15] Yet, I'd never personally experienced it. Was it true?

CHAPTER 6

NO CURRICULUM LEFT BEHIND

Wolfe-ish change occurred in my profession about sixteen years ago that opened the door for a profound shift in who determines standards and curriculum.

Our second grade team leader stopped me at the door of my classroom one afternoon in 2005. The Colorado sun was streaming in through partially open window blinds, but it was a slightly chilly day. It was about to get colder. She'd just been in a meeting and her face was twisted in concern. She hesitated, and my heart sank as it became clear she had bad news. Bluntly, she relayed the message: Kindergarten through second grade would no longer be allowed to teach science and social studies and it was implied that any extras like art had to go, too. She looked at me, incredulous herself. No Child Left Behind[16] (NCLB) legislation had passed at the federal level in 2002 but had yet to trickle its way down deeply into all schools. It takes an incredible amount of time, money, and effort to implement mandates that aren't local.

Supposedly, we only had time for reading, writing, and math in second grade because NCLB mandates and subjects-to-be-tested left no time for "extras." The years I'd spent merrily rolling along teaching, laughing, and learning with my students, had run smack dab into the policies and agendas of far-away education do-gooders. Mr. Wolfe knows full well that distance has a way of augmenting power,[17] but I didn't know what level of involvement he had in NCLB.

I felt like I was in a fog. I knew NCLB had passed, but no district official thoroughly explained it to us. Should I have researched NCLB on my own? Or, was it really the district's responsibility to educate its teachers on federal policy updates? Teachers were merely told to start—or stop— teaching a certain way or begin collecting data differently. No one gave us a full picture of what was expected of us and our schools, they just dictated new and different things we had to do. When we asked, "Why are we doing this? What's going on?" our questions were met with a wave of the hand and, "Oh, you know, that law that passed . . ."

What was I to do? I was under the direction of administrators who now lived in a test scores pressure cooker. Still, at the time, I didn't understand that schools could be closed and funding lost under this new federal mandate. I adopted a disgruntled attitude toward NCLB without fully understanding it. Slowly, the dusty churning of a battle instigated by federal mandate erased the breezy days of joyful teaching.

Looking back now, I see what a pivotal, defining moment the command to stop teaching certain subjects truly was. I was slow to understand that NCLB contained accountability and transparency stipulations. It also provided parents an opportunity to take their child to a different school if their local school was failing. Testing was one way to hold schools accountable, and annual school report cards provided transparency to what was taking place inside school walls. Wasn't that a good thing? I believed it was.

Yet while the George W. Bush administration toasted their perceived educational improvement success, one organization set out to stop and destroy it. As Rod Paige, former Secretary of Education and author of *The War Against Hope,* put it, ". . . accountability and transparency are anathema to union leaders."[18] While instructional expectations were changing, unions spread the message of apprehension about the tests to teachers.

I don't think any teacher or administrator in my building ever truly understood NCLB. We just followed the directives given to us. Well, mostly. My second-grade teaching teammates and I balked at the idea of not teaching science or social studies (parents, I figured, were never told the district had ended instruction in these subjects). We taught it anyway, surreptitiously. The hair on the back of my neck would be on end and sweat on my brow as I taught, expecting Mr. Wolfe at any moment. I was so afraid of being "caught" teaching art, science, or social studies. Under NCLB, these subjects were an implicit no-no in primary grades. I chalked up this nonsense to Mr. Wolfe, not knowing who else to blame.

But we also buckled down to devour professional development courses, striving to be experts in the best instructional methodologies. The district finally provided opportunities for teachers who needed courses to attain the status of "Highly Qualified." The thought of a poor annual school report card—an evaluation of our entire school as a whole—made us bristle. Data was no match for our analytical skills, and it informed the direction of our teaching, as did the tests. Testing time was torture. The pressure cooker atmosphere sucked all the air out of the school and left us pruned and shriveled, but our school was preserved by annual growth year after year. Our hard work paid off and thankfully, we earned decent annual school report card scores.

In spite of the difficulties of testing, it led to improved pedagogical practice. We clamored to receive back test scores, secretly grading ourselves and comparing our performance to that of our colleagues. We exalted when scores were high, moaned when they weren't, and despaired when we couldn't pinpoint the cause of plateaus. Would anyone ever perceive how NCLB caused schools to improve because of the new accountability to parents? My school was at the top of its game; we'd become better teachers.

We settled in to implementing updated state standards under NCLB. I had learned to accept the changes it brought (what else could I do?) while sticking to the belief that educational decisions should come from local stakeholders, namely parents and teachers, not the federal government.

Our sleeves were rolled up, we were dirty with effort, and following our *individual* state's standards. While we begrudged the admonition to ignore some subjects, we grew confident in our ability to help students progress. By default, I adopted ambivalence toward NCLB. I was focused on a class of twenty-something immediate concerns right in front of me.

With all of the NCLB requirements on our shoulders, we also tolerated Mr. Wolfe's ever-present buzzing about how awful the lack of funding for NCLB and all the new testing was for kids, teachers, and schools. The repeated sting of that message gave teachers and the public a negative attitude toward NCLB. "Keep the pressure on, with different tactics and actions, and utilize all events of the period for your purpose," Mr. Wolfe would advise.[19] By fighting for eight years to get the courts to rule federal education mandates must be federally funded, he paved the way for *his* agenda to one day be federally implemented and financed. NCLB left a mark on the education system, but Mr. Wolfe managed to lessen its impact via negative messaging and legal battles about funding.[20] Eventually, the funding battle was won in court. He didn't want schools and teachers to do well; he wished they do things *his* way. And he wished the federal government to pay for it.

Then like a blind-sided jolt from a bumper car, another federal program smacked teachers at full speed through a convulsion of changes. Mr. Wolfe had received his wish.

CHAPTER 7

NATIONAL ACADEMIC STANDARDS

"Goodbye, have a good summer!" Teachers and staff were calling up and down the hallways—except our vice principal. She passed hurriedly, rolling her eyes. She mumbled something about having to work with other district administrators on a big project that had suddenly come along. A lot of grant money was available but they had to act fast to get the application in on time. Her few seconds of hesitation registered deeply and set off alarm bells in my head. Something was not right; I just didn't know what it was. I bet Mr. Wolfe knew. I shrugged and skipped happily off to summer vacation, wishing her the best despite the stress she was exhibiting. Little did I know the upheaval of what students would be expected to learn and teachers expected to teach was about to crash like a tsunami through my profession.

Soon enough, I learned what she'd been working on. All the blood, sweat, and tears of states creating individual standards had been dumped down the drain so governors could freely accept $250 million dollars.[21] The Obama Administration's 2010 Race to the Top[22] was in full swing.

The trouble was, teachers were "in the trenches" teaching, and no one told them—or parents—what was going on. The shift to Common Core "State" Standards (CCSS) was *expected*—as if mandated. *Now.*

Back in June 1993, Massachusetts passed the Massachusetts Education Reform Act which, ". . . shall establish a set of statewide educational goals for all public elementary and secondary schools."[23]Jim Stergios, executive director of the Pioneer Institute, recalls the public hearings, debates, and discussions that took place over many years to refine and shape Massachusetts' individual state standards.[24] Massachusetts' journey to create solid frameworks for student learning took over a decade and included parent and teacher input. After all the effort by so many people, with public inclusion and commentary, Massachusetts chucked it all in 2009 because ". . . adoption and dissemination of standards for college and career readiness was a key component of our $250 million Race to the Top grant."[25]

Most states, including Colorado and Oregon, also exchanged state-developed standards for the Common Core standards. It was as though a stork had come and plopped the latest education reform on our desks. Why didn't anyone consult with parents and teachers about these matters? There we were, pulling all-nighters and changing the dirty diapers of someone else's illegitimate educational-reform baby. Again.

I carved out time to research the origins of the CCSS. It was like peeling layers of the most pungent of onions—each layer produced more tears. I learned that the Race to the Top money offered as part of the Obama Administration's stimulus package came at the time America was experiencing the Great Recession. Some saw the stimulus as a reprieve from the economic downturn, but Mr. Wolfe saw it as an opportunity to gain control. States were hard-pressed to meet their budgets. To say that states voluntarily agreed to adopt the CCSS was an oversimplification. They were too greedy for funds or too beholden to Mr. Wolfe to examine CCSS closely. The Race to the Top grant money was offered June 2, 2010. Applications were due August 10, 2010.[26] Within that short timeframe, states *had* to agree to the terms and conditions of the CCSS to receive the money . . . or miss out entirely.

I suppose it was natural to initially think that national standards (meaning CCSS) would be a good idea; we'd all be on the same page. After all, NCLB had created some positive changes in the areas of accountability and teacher qualifications, despite its constitutionally errant federal origin. (The Constitution leaves educational decisions to each state.) Although it took me awhile to see that the adequate yearly progress model in NCLB had it right—it gave teachers the flexibility to improve students' skills and show growth based on each child's uniqueness—it also left states' individual standards intact with at least some localized input. However, with CCSS, I felt robbed of a voice and professional autonomy, and parents had been sidelined. Mr. Wolfe had scored a kill; the victims were parent and teacher decisions about what kids would learn.

Parents, teachers, and school boards didn't have a chance against what Mr. Wolfe had been scheming for some time behind closed doors. When the opportunity arose to implement his design for the nation's education system through partnerships with key progressive Democrat leaders, he took it, of course.

The massive CCSS curricular changes came along just a few years before I decided to leave Colorado and return to Oregon. I was feeling burdened with heartache over changes in my profession, a recent breakup, and for others in extremely difficult situations. Should I be doing more than "just" teaching?

While spending time in prayer, God gave me an insightful understanding. I envisioned myself on a home construction site, painting the side of a house; however, I kept putting down my brush and hammering nails, affixing a switch plate, or rolling out carpet. I scrambled to be everywhere that needed work. God came along and said, "Kate? Didn't I ask you to paint the siding? I've assigned each person a job. If you don't stick to what I assigned you, you will become fatigued and unable to do the job I need you to do. Each person has a role that matches the specific talent I gave to them. When everyone fulfills their role, the whole house gets built! So please, just paint the siding."

"Use the abilities I have given you to do your work well, to the utmost of your ability and for my glory. *Just paint the siding,*" God admonished me. I couldn't yet see all the reasons he needed me to remain in public education. I had to trust. Since God had been faithful to me in the past, I knew I could rely on Him for strength and continue to teach.

Only glimpses of a swishing Wolfe tail through the public education trees made me think a collision of my beliefs and my professional requirements might be on the horizon. Federally mandated education policies served only to drive a wedge between parents and their children; this wasn't in line with my beliefs about family. God intended fathers and mothers to be responsible for their children in all areas, especially education. A system that supplanted this responsibility was untenable. Clearly, Mr. Wolfe and I didn't see eye-to-eye.

I spent quite a bit of time learning the new Common Core Standards, naturally comparing them to the state standards to which I was accustomed. Some of the language and terminology was unfamiliar, a new twist on colloquial "teacher talk." Confusion and questions arose. Why line plots? What happened to standard algorithms? What is "shades of meaning"? My constant refrain was, "I don't understand all this!" I asked for help interpreting the meaning of some CCSS standards. More than once, I was told to go look up online what they meant but never found a resource that clarified my confusion.

Later, I learned that at the March 2010 Massachusetts Board of Education meeting, Jason Zimba, one writer of the Common Core standards, admitted that the math standards are subpar: "The definition of college readiness,

I think it's a fair critique that it's a minimal definition of college readiness. Well, for the colleges most kids go to but not that most parents probably aspire . . . it's not for selective colleges,"[27] when taking a question about their sufficiency for college readiness. Dumbing down of American education was not a joke, but a sick reality. My stomach soured.

Deciphering Common Core came along just before navigating new discipline policy expectations. I needed to balance the requirements of daily teaching with the realities of chronic pain, but like meeting other challenges in life, I bulldozed ahead. I tried to lean into Jesus's comfort and count my blessings.

Among those blessings were (and still are) my students. I recall one unit lesson that added to my growing concern about the CCSS skills. The dim natural light and the glow from the projector revealed the furrowed brows of my third graders. I was guiding them through a word problem that, I began to discern, had spatial/visual area calculations formerly taught in a later grade. They'd been placed here in the name of "rigor" I supposed. The students were attentive, struggling to grasp the new concept, but frustration burst forth. The spatially complex area problem involved irregular shapes and missing side lengths; it was too abstract for most third-grade brains. Colleagues were expressing the same concerns; the CCSS were an egregious departure from developmental appropriateness.

So, we adapted. We had to. Our students would be tested on their capability with these standards. All new tests had been developed by two national companies and named the Smarter Balanced Assessment Consortium (SBAC) and the Partnership for Assessment of Readiness for College and Careers (PARCC). The tests were like an intimidating wolf pack keeping teachers in line. Unlike NCLB tests, which aligned with individual states' standards, all students nationwide took one of these tests, depending on which region they lived in. Just as the standards themselves, it removed local control and forced a nationalized curriculum. Mr. Wolfe's silence regarding the tests' development was suspicious.

I modified and adjusted where I could and used what I knew as an experienced teacher to be solid pedagogy (the method and practice of teaching) even when the standards departed from it. I rewrote the standards in kid friendly "I can" statements. I learned the third and fourth grade standards inside and out. I led a committee to develop district report cards based on the standards. When they were finalized, I wanted to puke.

Why on God's green earth are fourth graders expected to master *line plots?* Why are *third* graders asked to analyze information from multiple nonfiction sources then use that information to support their written *fiction* piece? Why I am being told that rote memorization of math facts is *bad?* I regretted my stamp of approval on the district's CCSS-based report cards, for it was all at once sickeningly clear to me that the CCSS were deeply flawed.

The Common Core standards assume every child is the same. There is no flexibility and no chance for teachers to showcase the growth they have fostered over the course of a school year. Wayne Brasler, veteran journalism teacher at the University of Chicago Lab Schools, put it this way, "This is a highly diverse nation. We have people growing up in the heart of very big cities, people who will never be in a big city; people on farms, people on reservations . . . People coming to school at the age of 4½ or 5 never having seen an orange or a rabbit . . . And, the waffle plate is being put over them and they're supposed to learn."[28]

My stomach turned at the realization I'd been had by Mr. Wolfe. I had been a pawn in the national standards scheme and carried it out unwittingly. He'd used my drive to do what is right, my pursuit of excellence in teaching, and twisted it for his own ends: utter control of what was taught, along with when and how, across the nation's entire education system. How could we let this happen? For years now teachers have been walking around, diligently teaching the Common Core standards like automatons. Mr. Wolfe was slick, preaching, ". . . the organizer will have a pretty good idea of what the [teachers] should be doing, and he will want to suggest, maneuver, and persuade the [teachers] toward that action."[29] We'd been maneuvered.

CHAPTER 8

WHO'S BEHIND THE NATIONAL ACADEMIC STANDARDS?

Once while in Bowling Green, Kentucky, I stayed at Hotel Sync. Its forward-thinking owners combined earth-friendly and guest-friendly accommodations. When I expressed my hope for more Hotel Sync locations, the owner shook his head no. As most businessmen know and understand, if you are not the one present at the site of business and able to ensure quality service yourself, it is difficult to maintain consistent quality. Hotel Sync's owners understood they were the best ones to deliver their exceptional brand of service; having hotels far away with the same high standards would be nearly impossible. The same axiom can be applied to the idea of the Common Core standards. The people close to the work—parents, teachers, and students—should be the ones designing and implementing new standards. Any standards dictated from a distant source will inevitably fail in meeting local needs and sustaining quality.

I kept peeling the CCSS onion. They'd been purposely labeled as "state" standards, a ploy to divert the public from figuring out they came from a centralized federal source. (Mr. Wolfe knew the general public was opposed to national standards.) "By 2011, 45 states had officially adopted the Common Core standards. Yet, by 2013, 62 percent of Americans said they had 'never heard of the Common Core.' "[30] This revealed that the CCSS hadn't been developed locally nor adequately explained to parents. Had they been, it would've made local newspaper headlines and garnered other media attention, just as Massachusetts' deliberations over standards did. Where had the standards originated, and who actually had a say?

Achieve, an independent, nonprofit education reform organization founded in 1996 by "leading governors and business leaders" partnered with the National Governors Association (NGA) and the Council of Chief State School Officers (CCSSO) in 2009 and began writing the CCSS.[31] The NGA is a 501(c)(3) nonprofit that purports to be, "[T]he voice of the nation's governors and one of the most respected public policy organizations in the country." It is a private organization started in 1908, and membership is optional.[32] The CCSSO is ". . . a nonpartisan, nationwide, nonprofit organization of public officials who head departments of elementary and secondary education in the states."[33] Are these entities the best source of standards for our students?

In the spring of 2010, the National Education Association (NEA) "agreed to become partners with the NGA and CCSSO."[34] Did teachers know of this partnership?

The Achieve staff writers worked under the title "Student Achievement Partners," which was ". . . founded by David Coleman, Susan Pimentel, and Jason Zimba, lead writers of the Common Core State Standards in literacy and mathematics." Philip Daro and William McCallum were also CCSS writers.[35] Jason Zimba, Philip Daro, and William McCallum are or were university professors with no K-12 teaching experience.[36] Susan Pimental and David Coleman didn't have K-12 teaching experience either. It was just like Mr. Wolfe to go outside the experience of his foe by using those so far removed from day-to-day public schooling—I was puzzled that he'd consider teachers with actual K-12 teaching experience as an enemy.[37] What was he hiding in these Common Core Standards?

The Achieve website, achieve.org, claims the CCSS were a "voluntary state-led effort."[38] *Why*, I pondered, *did no trails regarding the origination of the standards lead back to fifty separate state committees, conferences, or public teacher/parent discussion groups and meetings like those Massachusetts had used?* Better to call them National Standards than State Standards.

After the writers finished the standards, they passed them off to a "validation committee" of thirty people. Sandra Stotsky, professor of emerita at University of Arkansas, was one of those people. Stotsky is experienced in statewide standards development; she led Massachusetts' efforts in the '90s and early 2000s. Of her validation committee experience she says, "We had to sign a confidentiality agreement that we would not ever discuss what took place in the meeting itself."[39] She was concerned about the secrecy considering public matters should involve *the very public* that they would affect. Furthermore, when she and four others on the committee refused to sign off on validation, their refusal was publicly ignored; the public reports said that "everyone" on the committee agreed the standards were well done.

"Five out of 30 is a large number considering the fact that we were under enormous pressure to sign on. The five people who didn't agree to sign the letter simply were expunged from the record," recounts Jim Milgram, another dissenting validation committee member.[40] This made it easy for proponents to say *everybody* approved. Mr. Wolfe had failed to get 100% compliance, so he attempted to cover his tracks.

It had been naive for me to trust that states sent teachers and parents to meet and hash out the new standards in a process similar to what Massachusetts had done. States were "invited" to "voluntarily" *adopt* the already written standards. I felt as betrayed as Little Red Riding Hood. Teachers are hardworking and dedicated, yet our experience and expertise apparently meant nothing. It was a gut punch; teachers and parents had been blackballed out of the process of creating the *very standards* they would have to implement daily.

My initial, accepting naiveté regarding the CCSS had turned sour in part because of piloting the Smarter Balanced Assessment (SBAC), the test of CCSS mastery, with my third graders. It was too much for them. Just as the standards were developmentally inappropriate, so was the length and format of the test. I learned too late that my SBAC pilot-test feedback was unwanted. Teacher input didn't matter; we were powerless in the jaws of Mr. Wolfe. I feared the feedback given by the teachers during the standards review may have received the same treatment. I wondered. . . was there actual teacher review and approval at all? As I continued to peel back more layers, I discovered who the approvers were:

- The American Federation of Teachers (AFT), in 2010, resolutely affirmed advocacy of the standards.[41] Which of their teachers had seen the standards? And how many had seen them?

- Groups of teachers from the NEA and the AFT were asked to look over the standards between June 2009 and March 2010.[42] The unions then signed letters of agreement with the standards.[43] Which teachers? How many?

- Barbara Kapinus of the NEA oversaw member teacher feedback regarding the new standards.[44] National education policy directors for the NEA and the AFT had frequently met with the standards' writers at Student Achievement Partners.[45] Oh, to be a fly on the wall!

It can safely be assumed that neither the NEA nor the AFT director told the writers to stop for the sake of the millions of other union members—who were teachers—who had not yet heard of the standards. Teachers who know kids' developmental needs. Teachers who have actual

K-12 classroom experience. Teachers for whom the NEA and AFT are supposed to represent and be the voice.[46]

The teachers involved in reviewing the standards were National Board Certified, but it is unclear how many were involved or which grade levels were represented. Nationalized teacher certification accentuates the tearing away of local control; how could local parents and local teachers trust *national* standards looked over by *"national"* teachers, who may teach anywhere in the nation? How thorough was their review? Was a *review* of the standards by "national" teachers as meaningful as *local* teachers *writing* the standards?[47] I was certain that premature wrinkles were going to start forming on my forehead thanks to a consistent squint of disbelief.

An NEA policy brief from 2010 included this: "Parents and communities will need time to become familiar with the CCSS . . ." That same brief said, "Policy needs to take into account all the factors that are involved in developing a *new education system* [emphasis mine] . . ."[48] All I could conclude was that the teachers unions had been complicit in developing and approving the CCSS and then, when parents and teachers revolted against the standards, unions did an about-face and pointed fingers of blame at poor state and district level "implementation" and "lack of teacher training."

When it became clear to me that once again entities far removed from the proper triangle of education stakeholders (parents, students, and teachers) were butting in, I felt a burden to protect my students' parents from this usurpation of decisions about their own children's education. I also wanted to protect teachers. Agitation over the origins of the standards and what it meant for families gnawed at me like a tree at the mercy of a beaver. If no one was seeking input from teachers in each locale, let alone parent input, what could I do? I felt boxed in. How was I to conduct myself, knowing the origin of the Common Core standards we'd been asked to use lay with a company no teacher had ever heard of, but Mr. Wolfe knew so well? "In your anger do not sin," reads Ephesians 4:26.[49] Couldn't God see how this was affecting kids, their parents, and teachers?

I feared speaking up, wrongly—or rightly—perceiving my colleagues were content to make whatever changes asked of them in their pedagogy and plod ahead. After all, Mr. Wolfe wasn't telling them to complain about the standards themselves, just the implementation. Whatever that meant. Would they really continue to be maneuvered, even though we all shared concerns about these standards? I'm ashamed at my previous inability to gather enough courage to push back harder against what I knew to be poor quality standards and pedagogy for kids. I should've done was what right, but Mr. Wolfe's constant message to teachers was "don't rock the boat." No one wanted to be the naysayer who got thrown overboard. That would be too shameful.

Later in my research, I came across a 2015 article in the Oregon teachers union magazine, *Today's OEA*. The OEA is an affiliate of the NEA who, just five years prior, had given glowing approval to the standards. Now the tone was derisive of the CCSS, explaining the work groups that had been part of making the standards by saying, "Out of 66 people, there was only one teacher in each group." It went on to include an insult of corporate involvement in the CCSS, "The Gates Foundation gave over $200 million to promote the creation and adoption of the Common Core in 2013 alone."[50] So maybe the union was not complicit in the CCSS? Then I noticed the article omitted the NEA's partnership with the creators of the standards, as well as the fact the NEA was one recipient of Gates Foundation funds. I was perplexed.

With money the NEA accepted from the Gates Foundation for their Master Teacher project, Chicago teachers were asked to begin using the Common Core standards and create lessons to go with them.[51] It was like the spider inviting a fly into her parlor. By 2014 the Chicago teachers were adamantly opposed to the Common Core. But they had to keep using it, as did most of the rest of us, because many states had accepted the terms of the Race to the Top deal: money in exchange for using the CCSS.[52] I hung my head. Why hadn't I been told other teachers across the nation were dissatisfied with CCSS? Why weren't our concerns being heard?

If the teachers unions had been busily partnering with the NGA, CCSSO, and other creators of the standards and developing a "new education system," why hadn't they included *all* teachers from the outset? More importantly, I wondered why they hadn't *opposed* standards that *weren't written by teachers?* The CCSS were codified when former President Obama signed into law the current Every Student Succeeds Act.

Mr. Wolfe? Is that you?

As I wavered on whether or not to speak out against the CCSS, Jesus's words echoed in my mind: "Why are you so afraid? . . . Do you still have no faith?"[53]

CHAPTER 9

COMPREHENSIVE SEXUALITY EDUCATION

Throughout my school years, my dad was on the local school board. Thus began my other education; the one supplied by my dad's exclamations of frustration with the public school system, curriculum, and teacher negotiations. This was augmented with literature coming into our home such as the *Phyllis Schlafly Report, Focus on the Family,* and the like. These spoke to the importance of the *nuclear family* being the bedrock of any society. They promoted a sound commitment to God, marriage of one man and one woman, and loyalty to and defense of the United States of America and her freedoms. Limited government overreach, especially as pertained to schooling, was also expounded upon.

One policy that came before the school board while I was in third grade was the Safe Touch program. This was an attempt to help children know the difference between appropriate, healthy familial affection, and abuse. At the time, it appeared Mr. Wolfe seemed genuinely concerned with kids' well-being.

The Safe Touch program of the eighties now looks innocuous compared to the comprehensive sexuality education (CSE) being written into law in many states. I plunged into research as soon as I heard about CSE from a fellow teacher in another state. It would be coming to Oregon, I reasoned, so I should dig around. I was jaded by prior experiences with teachers being the last to know but the first expected to deliver strangers' programs to students. So, I wasn't shocked that by the time I conducted my research, CSE had been law in Oregon for *two years.* Not only had I *never* heard about committees for creating CSE standards—or plans for implementation of such materials—but I was *never* informed the items had become *law.* Teachers obviously had no voice in policy and neither did parents.

It didn't take much effort for me to locate the Oregon Health Education Standards online.[54] In California and Oregon, comprehensive sexuality education ideas hide behind innocent-sounding monikers like "Healthy Youth Act"[55] and "Health Education Standards."[56] *Kindergartners* are taught to "identify sources of support to seek information about sexual and reproductive health." They are also taught to "recognize that there are many ways to express gender." Fifth graders are expected to "explain differences and similarities of how individuals identify regarding gender or sexual orientation." Seventh graders must "compare factors that may influence condom use and other safer sex decisions" and "analyze factors that can affect the ability to

give or perceive the provision of consent to sexual activity."
High schoolers "access medically accurate information and
resources about pregnancy, pregnancy options, including
parenting, abortion, adoption, and prenatal care services."

Planned Parenthood often designs curriculum
materials to teach these concepts.[57] It seems logical for an
organization such as Planned Parenthood to encourage
sexually risky behavior, since they profit from such activity.
The curriculum advertises it's about reducing sexually
transmitted diseases, sexual violence, and unintended
pregnancies. They even throw in the word *abstinence* a few
times.

I grieved while reading the CSE standards. Doing
what is right and honorable is nonexistent, but pursuing
one's own desires as long as the other person "consents" is
lauded. How could I teach such ideas when my own faith
calls me to "Be devoted to one another in love. Honor one
another above yourselves?"[58] and believe that "God created
mankind in his own image, in the image of God he created
them; male and female he created them."[59]

Mr. Wolfe has a knack for clothing rotten ideas in "moral
garments."[60] I shuddered, imagining myself standing in
front of innocent-faced students, being expected to say
words like . . . Honestly, I can't even type them here. Or
teach them to "recognize sources of medically accurate
information about human sexual and reproductive anatomy
. . ." *I am not their parent.* I teach reading, writing, math,
science, and social studies and barely have time to squeeze
in all that.

Now would I be expected to teach them, in coed company nonetheless, how to "demonstrate on an anatomical model how to perform genital exams"?[61] If I taught 11- and 12-year-olds, I'd be expected to have them "define sexual violence" and "identify the steps to correctly use a condom." None of this sounds like ethical behavior for a teacher. In fact, the standards and accompanying curriculums sound more like the activities of sex offenders who groom their victims. Sexual conduct as defined under Oregon Revised Statute 339.370 is conduct: "sexual in nature, directed toward a K-12 student, interferes with educational performance and creates an offensive educational environment."[62] I would soon be asked to say and do things in my classroom that would be sexually abusive in any other context. How could teachers reconcile the requirement to teach sexually explicit material while following proper conduct guidelines? Much less a teacher committed to following Biblical precepts.

A video on StopCSE.org includes Michelle Cretella, MD. She states, "As president of the American College of Pediatricians, I am deeply concerned about comprehensive sexuality education for four reasons: First, it sexualizes children. Second, it threatens children's health. Third, it promotes a dangerous gender ideology. And fourth, it undermines the parent-child relationship, which violates parental rights."[63]

Where did the CSE come from? Just as with the CCSS approvals, Mr. Wolfe is behind the CSE as well. The CSE standards are essentially the same throughout all states that have adopted them. I discovered there is uniformity because states are not writing their own "health" standards, but merely copying the national template. Multiple organizations, one being the National Education Association's Health Information Network (NEAHIN), wrote National Sexuality Education Standards (NSES) in 2012.[64] In 2020, they released a second edition of these standards.[65] These form the basis for comprehensive sexuality education. A cursory visit to the NSES website will only show the outer moral-looking garments. A deeper look at the standards and curriculums will reveal that five-year-olds will be taught to "recognize that there are many ways to express gender."[66] What happens to a child's psyche if told they were "born in the wrong body" as the trending phrase goes?

Would New Business Item #47 of the NEA 2019 National Assembly be considered sexual in nature and directed toward a K-12 student? "NEA will work with current partners (such as GLSEN), to expand on the number of professional development opportunities for Gender Sexuality Alliance (GSA) advisors?"[67] GLSEN is the Gay, Lesbian, Straight Education Network and one coauthor of the 2020 National Sexuality Education Standards.[68]

The partnership between GLSEN and the NEA caused me chagrin. The CSE standards clearly digress from Biblical foundations, which teachers of faith such as myself choose to follow. In our culture, promiscuity and sexual deviations are increasingly acceptable. Adults make their own choices in these areas, some acting as Mr. Wolfe would: choosing ethics as he goes to suit his passions. Jesus-followers seeking to abide by Biblical directives are mocked and scorned for their abstinence and commitment to heterosexual marriage.

CSE was the most contentious of all topics I'd come across.

Let it not be forgotten, however, that these "healthy standards" are not being written for adults with fully developed prefrontal cortexes—but for *children,* ages three to eighteen. And promoted *not* by the great teachers in this nation, but by Mr. Wolfe, aka *the teachers unions.*

Ashamedly, that is the organization that scared me. *I must reach deep into understanding the full meaning of "Greater love has no one than this: that someone lay down his life for another,"*[69] *if I am to open myself up to the sharp ridicule and decimation of my public teaching career that the union is capable of meting out to those teachers who dare speak against their agenda.*

Would I lay down my life for the sake of America's students?

─────── CHAPTER 10 ───────
A ONE-YEAR LEAVE OF ABSENCE

I t was late spring when I decided to take a one-year leave of absence during the following 2017-2018 school year. One night I stopped short, toothbrush suspended in midair, and leaned against the bathroom wall. *Was it feasible to step away from school for a year?* I worried. God was stretching my faith. I could look back over my life and make a long list of how God had protected me and provided for me yet choosing to walk away from teaching and a paycheck seemed insurmountable. Would I trust Him and step away?

I'd always loved school as a child and knew from a very young age that I wanted to be a teacher. While friends wondered what to do with their lives, I never wavered in my love for kids, learning, and teaching. God had gifted me to teach. "Before you were born, I set you apart."[70]

Right then, however, I was exasperated. My colleagues and I were undervalued and unrecognized while shouldering stressful day-to-day school environments. We felt uneasy and left out of the decision-making loop. Teaching wasn't joyful anymore and teachers had no voice. My profession had changed, and not for the better, thanks to Mr. Wolfe's machinations behind the scenes. It was as painful as my all-too-familiar chronic pain episodes.

Although I would be out of the classroom, my heart would still be in education. My body would be travelling, but my mind would be puzzling out the troubles with the current system. It felt natural to step into the role of protector between them and my students. Could teachers regain our voice? Could we be empowered once more to partner with parents in directing policy?

I was determined to speak up about the issues consuming public schools with clenched teeth and ready to take any opposing hits. So, decision made, I packed the car with a laptop, voice recorder, theories about the causes of problems in education, and sped off around the United States of America to ask teachers their perspective on the public education system. I wanted to know what other educators understood about the changes in public education. Was Mr. Wolfe breathing down their necks, too? Did they understand who Mr. Wolfe really was: The seemingly benign teachers unions disguised as advocates for teachers.

Was Terry Moe, author of *Special Interest*, correct when he explained, "What the rise of the teachers unions has meant in the grander scheme of things, for all of us, is a radical shift in the structure of power in American education, and with it the emergence of what amounts to a new type of education system for the modern era."[71]

Who, exactly, are the teachers unions?

It was no accident that I read *Feisty and Feminine*, by Penny Nance, president of Concerned Women for America, in May of 2017 before I set out on my road trip. After reading it, I knew it was a prerequisite to some series of events toward which God was leading me. On pages thirteen and fourteen of Nance's book, she references the Old Testament and the life of Esther, wife of King Xerxes, ruler of the Persian Empire: "Though it could have cost Esther her position, her power, even her very life, she trusted that God had raised her up for a reason, and by finding her voice and speaking up, she saved herself and her people. We too were born 'for such a time as this.' "[72]

Nance's book filled me with hope and inspiration. I knew that the hard path of teaching my colleagues about the teachers union, the intimidating Mr. Wolfe, was the right one. " 'Esther Women,' Nance encouraged, 'this is your chance to find your voice. In whatever sphere of influence the Lord gives you, you can choose to be a light for the things that are right and true.' "[73] All through the years, God was molding and shaping my faith in Him. He'd brought me to this point of opportunity to lift my voice and champion a cause. If I leaned fully into Jesus's repeated admonition that He'd never leave or forsake me, would I fall or be held up?[74] I was beginning to see that he would indeed hold me up. After all, God had seen me through other difficult times such as heartbreaks and being separated from family. It would be difficult to gain the listening ear of colleagues so accustomed to hearing only the unions' messages. It felt like a fool's mission, but courage was bubbling up from strength supplied through faith in God.

While waiting for travel arrangements to fall into place, I spent time gathering all the information I could on teachers unions. I'd followed the *Friedrichs vs. California Teaching Association*[75] case, interested in why a teacher would take the union to court. I was in awe of Rebecca Friedrich's bravery and hoped someday I could meet her in person. I gathered a stack of books, including all perspectives of education and teachers unions, and began reading voraciously. It became clear the teachers unions were prominent in public education decision-making.

When President John F. Kennedy's executive order 10988 of 1962 approved public employee collective bargaining at the federal level, and unions got their wish for a federal Department of Education granted by President Jimmy Carter in 1980, teachers unions' power exploded. States had begun approving public employee bargaining as early as 1959, and joined with the law-backed ability to mandatorily collect dues from teachers' paychecks, unions had the money and status to decide all things education.

On the surface, it may seem as though the connections of the union to discipline policies, Common Core, and comprehensive sexuality education are simply innocent partnerships where *others* are calling the shots. Unions have succeeded in making it look like education changes come from somewhere else (voluntary state-led efforts, teacher advocacy, and parent-teacher association approvals). They've got the connections, wealth, and power to do just that. I had a hunch most teachers weren't acquainted with this reality.

Academics and researchers, nonprofit liberal and conservative groups alike have posted articles regarding teachers unions. The unions themselves have healthy websites and bloggers throw in their two cents, no problem. Professors and research institutions had written on the topic. A former secretary of education had written about unions and so had a charter school principal. Searching for a book written by a teacher on the topic of teachers unions was like looking for a needle in a haystack. But at the time, there wasn't even a needle to find. It was easy to find books teachers have written about the history of education and classroom anecdotes. But what were teachers' perspectives about unions? How much did they know about the organizations to which they were giving $900–$1300 a year? [76] Was it possible that my fellow teachers didn't really know much? I had some knowledge of teachers unions from my dad; however, it had taken me months to search out and better understand them.

By the time the heat of July melted into August, I was itching to find out if teachers could answer questions about their own unions. A mix of delight about upcoming travel mixed with curiosity over what I might learn. My sabbatical would split into parallels, as though I were going on two journeys: one for relaxation and liberty and one for the sake of students, their parents, and the profession I love. I also fully expected to meet Mr. Wolfe along the way. On purpose. I had some questions.

CHAPTER 11

THE NOT-SO-SUBTLE
PRESSURE TO JOIN

O f all the fifty states I've witnessed, Oregon is still top of the list for beauty. On this particular day of my journey, I would be visiting with a former teacher, Nathan, who had also served on a school board. I'd been down his Oregon driveway before, and the impeccable landscaping, friendly trees, and welcoming flowers never got old. My knowledge of Mr. Wolfe was increasing and I wanted to know if other teachers knew of or felt his presence. I would soon discover the workings of Mr. Wolfe through teacher conversations, but the teachers themselves had no idea they were speaking a language he'd taught them.

Nathan began with a disclaimer after we'd settled into his living room: "[Unions had become] a force of manipulation through government agencies and [is] used for benefitting a few that are in power rather than taking care of those that are supplying the funds to that union." [77] He felt that instead of benefitting people, unions had taken a wrong turn somewhere along the way.

Nathan had begun his teaching career in California in the '60s, an era when union recruiting was blanketing the nation and states were deciding to permit, require, or prohibit collective bargaining following the push for *public* sector negotiations. At that time, joining (and therefore paying) was a choice. "They promised you if you did join, they would negotiate for bigger salaries. It was all about your income." Nathan didn't join, he explained while laughing smugly. "I was a penny pincher! I figured they didn't deserve any of the money that I worked for." I laughed along with him but winced at the thought of the roughly $5,000 I'd been forced to pay the union over seven years.

Nathan moved to Oregon four years later and began teaching there. He recalled the push to join a union in Oregon being two to four years behind the movement in California. Once again, joining or not was still a choice. It was the early '70s. By about the third year into his Oregon teaching job, however, the union representative in his district became "relentless in threatening you—daily—to make sure you joined." I was appalled to learn he'd been verbally intimidated on a *daily* basis.

At some point, Nathan had engaged the lever on his recliner and was speaking from a lounging position. I wondered if it felt good to express this angst to someone after all this time. All these years later, the lack of a looming union representative or fear of repercussions made the telling easier. "It was a personal thing to [the union rep]," Nathan continued, "that you weren't a good teacher unless you joined the group. So, it was something to decide whether you were a valuable person to education or you were supposed to be a reject because you didn't join the union. He would meet at lunch time and talk your ear off about how bad you were. It was always about you personally, that you were somebody holding up the progress from all of your fellow teachers." Nathan courageously resisted the pressure and never joined the union.

The personalized attacks Nathan experienced demonstrate the union use of "Alinsky tactics." Rod Paige, former United States Secretary of Education, commented in his book *The War on Hope,* that after the legalization of public sector collective bargaining, "The NEA totally discarded its century-old reputation as an organization dedicated to improving all facets of education through professional cooperation and learning . . . power politics was melded into the radical organization it became. By the 1970s, strikes were no longer a matter of righting wrongs or addressing grievances—the NEA viewed them as a means to an end. The most telling indicator of this shift occurred when the NEA began using Saul Alinsky as a consultant. Alinsky gained considerable fame as an organizer in the late 1960s and is perhaps best known for his book Rules for Radicals . . . Alinsky personally conducted intense training sessions with the NEA's field organizers (known as UniServ operatives) . . ."[78] Mr. Alinksy's ("Wolfe") ideology, outlined in his aforementioned book, is still used today by teachers unions to advance their cause.

"Pick the target, freeze it, personalize it . . ."[79] is a union-learned Alinsky tactic that was foisted on Nathan. How had he managed to hold up under such assault? This same targeting persists today from the unions but reveals itself more subtly. There is the unspoken assumption that everyone is joining, and you'd better too, or else risk condescending looks, snide remarks, and lonely lunch breaks. I'd been accused of sabotage by fellow teachers in an email, but friends of mine have endured the blunt force of screams, name-calling, and persistent contempt in face-to-face confrontations.

Aaron Benner, a Minnesota teacher who spoke out against lenient discipline practices in his district found out all too soon that district officials and his teachers union were not in his corner. They threw false accusations of misconduct at him and his union encouraged him to plead guilty, even though he had done nothing wrong.[80]

The hot flames of peer pressure and intimidation during initial union recruitment years have been veiled as smoldering coals today, ready to accuse and publicly humiliate. It's as though educators subconsciously accept joining the union as what supposedly keeps them from getting burned, not realizing administration and unions are intertwined, as Aaron found out.

Most teachers unquestioningly join a union, taking on the yoke of membership as if teaching isn't allowed without it. One new Oregon teacher told me, "I wasn't listening. I think I was playing on my cell phone," regarding the union orientation meeting he'd been required to attend. "I got a [free] t-shirt," he had added.[81] And a former Washington, D.C. teacher named Ava told me, "They don't actually explain what they're there for." Ava now resides in North Carolina and no longer teaches. "They just kinda tell you . . . it comes out of your check. I was told: This is what you do as a teacher."[82]

Is an "Alinksy" ends-justifies-the-means mentality appropriate for *anyone?* Would you accept this reasoning and behavior from your students if they wanted to cheat to get an A? After all, their goal is good grades. Yet unions are applying this philosophy today. For example, they justify creating a climate of fear among teachers about being sued to gain the end result of millions of dollars paid to them in dues.

Nathan experienced union ill treatment decades ago, and Anna [83] experienced it about three years ago: I met Anna on a cloud-darkened, damp night. Somehow the chilly evening and dodging puddles as I slipped in and out of the dimly lit coffee shop made me feel like a secret agent. Our meeting was brief and included her passing me a union newsletter meant for members only. If I'd had a trench coat and a fedora, surely I would've been labeled a union nonmember spy. Why was I afraid? I was on a mission, but I had no Captain America shield, bulging muscles, or Tom Cruise stunts. My call sign was *Incognito,* and with knowledge of Nathan's story and other scary instances of union tactics, under the radar was where I wanted to be right then.

Although, even in the midst of my fear, I could hear Jesus's words, "Do not fear."[84]

Once settled into our seats in the café, coffee in hand, Anna relayed her tale: "I signed up last year [for union membership] because a big, huge man came into one of our meetings last year and coerced me into signing. First of all, his size was intimidating, right? And everyone was saying, 'It's free. We're here to protect you!'...Things like that, those kind of hook words. I talked to other people; they felt coerced also. It sounded like we were already being charged for it, so, I didn't really understand the whole point in signing up for it if I'm already paying. I wasn't sure what was going on." Anna still sounded confused and frustrated. The "big, huge man" had also asked them if there were any problems at school. When someone spoke up, Anna felt he "seemed to be really pushy with that kind of thing . . . the person that said something felt like she was turning in our school."

"It felt really uncomfortable and not a safe place to be," Anna added. Why would a union rep treat my colleagues this way, making them feel so intimidated? Didn't the union claim to serve and protect them? My face remained as calm as possible. I could vent in the car on the way home. Anna went on to share about her work with a boy at school with whom she'd been instrumental in helping in profound ways. I was proud to know her, and so happy kids had *her* as their paraprofessional.

I was heartsick after that interview. The crinkled brow of concern I had at the beginning of my sabbatical year now looked more like Mrs. Potato Head™ with her "angry eyes."

When a union representative and school employee approached Dana, a school bus driver, Dana was hosing off a bus.[85] They just wanted to talk about union benefits and get her signed up. I knew Dana worked hard to support herself and children as a single mom. "I've already been seeing the dues taken out of my paycheck," Dana explained to the union representative. If the dues were being taken, why did Dana need to "sign up"? Why hadn't the union been around before dues were extracted to explain and sign her up then? It sounded similar to Anna's predicament. "All we have to do is get you signed up so you can reap the benefits of what you're already paying for," the rep told Dana. Dana had been working for over a year at that point with dues being extracted while she was a substitute bus driver. Was she *finally* going to get something for her money?

"Discounts on home insurance . . . you can save on your car insurance and you can save on your phone bill," Dana related some of the "benefits" of membership the rep talked about. "I've got a hose in my hand, grungy work clothes, and I don't want the soap to be drying on the bus," Dana told me. She was in a dilemma. It's not as though the representative was thoughtful about the where and when this was taking place. Dana internally wrestled with what to do, "I didn't have time to sit down and really, you know, hammer it out." What was she supposed to do? She's obviously busy and yet this union rep wants her to take the pamphlets and sign the card. So Dana did, figuring she could deal with it later.

I thought I knew so much before my interviewing began. The more I listened, the more questions I had. I'd never done such investigative work before. Suddenly being a "spy" made me feel I could do something heroic. My goal was not just to learn more about unions, but to bring educators and the public knowledge about what is really going on with teachers unions. My humble tools were an aged laptop, notebooks, and a tape recorder. What I lacked in equipment I made up for in zeal. I would need it for the roller coaster ride ahead. I chuckle at the mixed emotions I felt at first when speaking with teachers. I was racing to connect with them before the crush of school responsibilities buried them until winter break.

--------- CHAPTER 12 ---------

DUES OUT OF YOUR PAYCHECK

At the beginning of my leave of absence, the packing of my teaching supplies into storage coincided with running off to interview teachers. Wadded newspapers lay about half-full boxes. The packing tape roll always seemed near-empty. Talking with teachers was a welcome break from the packing, preparing, and waiting.

I could see the road stretched out ahead of me, but not around the bend. Every inch of travel was done in faith; the belief that God had prepared me for what was most certainly around the bend on my quest to right the perceived ills in my profession.

It was early August when I shuffled into an Oregon school to meet with Susan and a few of her coworkers. Susan[86] didn't know how much her union dues were that year. "[The union] just sent me something in the mail. It was something saying that if I wanted to opt out of the political portion of dues, that would be an option." Susan's mailer wasn't from the union, it was from the Freedom Foundation, an organization trying to reach teachers with information about their rights.

Surely some teachers knew where their dues went and the purpose of their union. One of Susan's colleagues called out, "It's broken down on your paystub," as to *how* union dues are spent. But her paystub merely showed *where* the money is sent: *local, state and national*. There are two main national unions, the NEA and AFT, with state affiliates and local affiliates. Accepting representation from NEA or AFT for your local union means accepting their requirement of affiliation with the state and national units.

The AFT is the smaller of the two and is an affiliate of the AFL-CIO. Its membership includes not just educators but other government workers at the federal, state, and local level as well as healthcare workers. It has 1.7 million members within 3,000 local affiliates nationwide.[87]

The NEA has affiliates at the state level in all fifty states, and affiliates in 14,000 "communities."[88] Those communities are local school districts. The NEA boasts a membership of approximately three million.

When I later analyzed responses of all the teachers I interviewed, most didn't understand where their dues were sent:

- "I bet they go national, then spread it out," said Tara, a first-year teacher.[89]
- "I really don't know," Nancy, a veteran teacher of over twenty-five years told me.
- "I don't know . . . I believe it went part to the state and part to the college itself," said Mary, an Oregon educator of over forty-three years.[90]

- "I'm gonna say . . . the local and state?" guessed Michelle, a veteran Pennsylvania teacher.
- "I don't know much about the details of how it is spent, I guess," said Ashley, a teacher for fifteen years in Oregon, who later became a union building representative so she'd be more informed about her union.[91]

I eventually ceased being surprised by the answers. In the 2015-16 school year, Oregon teachers in my district paid about $598 to the state affiliate, $185 to the national affiliate, and $117 stayed local. I've paid between $830 and $908 dollars per school year (even though I was a nonmember).

When the right to collectively bargain in the public sector became in vogue at the state level in the late '50s, it looked much like private sector bargaining. It mimicked the established private sector laws under the National Labor Relations Act of 1935. This included laws stipulating there be an exclusive representative. A majority vote of employees determines who becomes their exclusive representative. Only a union chosen by a majority of employees may receive certification—the right to represent all employees in the bargaining unit—even if a minority do not wish to be represented by the chosen union. However, choosing exclusive representative status may include affiliation at the local, state, and national level as a condition of representation.[92]

Teachers at Susan's school and teachers across the nation don't understand that the support they use is *local,* yet most of their dues are sent to the state and national offices.

Paystubs show what percentage is sent to the local, state, and national affiliate. When I asked the group of teachers if they'd be interested in paying seventy-five percent less in dues while retaining the same union benefits, they hesitated. How would that be possible? Very few know that the law allows teachers to decide who represents them, based on a majority vote. (It is possible for teachers to have independent or local-only unions, which I'll explain in later chapters.) There is no reason to fund or be affiliated with a state and national union. A simple, inexpensive, local-only union representation has all rights to collectively bargain.

Furthermore, most of those teaching now have never had a say in who their exclusive representative is. They've never voted for or against their union as the exclusive representative. Current unions were voted in before I entered kindergarten, and for the most part have not budged.

Local union affiliates provide "association" or" building" representatives (teachers who attend the local union meetings) for each school in a bargaining unit. These association representatives are present with teachers who want to have a serious conversation with their administration about an issue. Teachers call on association (union) representatives for assistance when grievances arise. Some association representatives receive a stipend, some do not. Local officers run meetings and socials, keep the employees updated on association business, and act as a liaison between management and employees. Members of the local unit are selected to be at the negotiations table. In short, the locals do all the heavy lifting but receive very little of the dues collected.

State union affiliates employ Uniserv representatives. These Uniserv workers are recruiters, lobbyists, and political activists that cover different regions in each state. They contribute to committees that draw up legislation to be introduced. They also see to it that each district makes decisions in common with other districts. For instance, a union-favored curriculum adopted in a district in the northwest corner of the state will find its way to the southeast corner of the state. "All the other districts are using it," the peer pressure goes. In the same vein, the army of Uniserv workers indirectly pressure school boards and persuade local union representatives to convince their districts to change, with the premise, "Well, you should adopt this policy because everyone else is." Local, autonomous, independent decision-making gets squashed, but the state-level union gets the largest share of dues and the biggest muscle.

National unions enjoy a seat at the cabinet level as they loiter around the Department of Education. Policy writing and introducing legislation are coupled with large amounts of lobbying. Political action and continuous exertion of power throughout the nationwide public education system are an implicit focus, financed by teacher dues. But do teachers know what policies the national unions are pushing? Do they agree with their distant national representation?

Educators are rightly focused on the day-to-day improvements of their school, but they often don't pay attention to the large portion of dues being automatically deducted from their paychecks each month. Who does? It's not as though we check each month to see how much Medicare and Social Security comes out; however, it may explain why a vast number of teachers cannot answer how much their dues are and don't notice how much they increase each year. Nor do they stop to consider what would be a reasonable amount.

Just how much do union services cost, anyway? Most teachers I spoke with said, "I don't know." "Gosh, probably thousands," Nicole said during our phone interview.[93] Hannah, another Oregon teacher, replied with, "I'm sure it is expensive."[94] What do contract negotiations look like in your district? Who is sitting at the table for educators? Lawyers? Uniserv representatives? Or teachers receiving a small stipend, if anything? Most teachers have never seen an audited union fiscal report. This suits the unions' ends just fine.

Amazingly, local union building/association representatives and local union officers (leaders in the local union such as president, secretary, etc.) don't know much more about their union. A small percentage of union members got cantankerous when I asked questions such as, "What do your teachers union dues pay for?" Is it because they don't know the answer?

I met Cindy,[95] a seasoned educator of thirty-five years, at a coffee shop. I wanted to know her thoughts on teachers unions because she was a former union association representative and current union committee member. She'd received five dollars for every union meeting she attended. We settled outside in the shade of the patio on a sunny summer day. Cindy began, "My assumption is that when my local reps go to the state meetings, they see the budget and they let me know about the state budget and they give input at the state and then national level on my behalf." I wondered if Cindy had seen a state budget or just heard a report on it. Clearly, she trusted her union to do right by her. She sipped her coffee and patiently answered my questions.

Cindy had good reasons for having faith in her union. She appreciated the informative union magazines and literature. She knew dues went to the local, state, and national affiliates. "[Bargaining] will cost more if [it] goes longer because people have to be free from the classroom . . . and there are legal advice expenses," she explained. "The union pays for substitutes in classrooms when negotiating happens during the day. Sometimes the union gives the members stipends to be on the bargaining team." I could tell Cindy appreciated having representation, but I chafed at the constraints of maintaining neutrality in interviews. I also wanted to have a longer conversation, but felt I had to stick to just interviewing.

After meeting with Cindy, I wondered if she'd seen the union brochure I had seen one day the previous year. No one else was in the teachers' lounge at the time and the school day was over. I'd stopped in to fill my water bottle. As I stood taking a long draft of cool water, I turned toward the door. There, in the middle of the union bulletin board, was a breakdown of dues spending from the Oregon Education Association, titled *Where Do Your Dollars Go?*[96] I'd asked that question when the union tried to recruit me four years prior and never received an answer. It was 2016. The brochure was for the 2014-2015 fiscal year. A few weeks later, I snuck a copy.

A chart delineated how the OEA used dues money. Bargaining and Legal Services received forty dollars of each teacher's state affiliate dues. That's all. The two main reasons teachers join and pay a union were the two services receiving the smallest amount of total revenue. My dues were almost $900. Unions are nonprofit organizations. What was happening to the rest of the money?

Total revenue for the year: $18,500,537. (Doesn't that fall in the definition of wealthy?) The General Fund received $530, which went to seven different "centers" within the state OEA office. The Governance and Administration centers combined used twenty-five percent of the general fund for association events, building maintenance and a photo copy center, to name a few. The Public Affairs center spent ten percent of total revenue. This spending included political action. The Legal Services center received just two percent of total revenue. Each center used seventy percent of their portion for "Salary, Auto Allowance, and Benefits." All I could infer was Oregon Education Association employees make more money and have more benefits than any teacher, anywhere. Ironically, none of this spending is necessary for teachers in a local school district to enjoy all the rights and protections afforded under public bargaining laws. Nor is it necessary to secure legal protections. How would Cindy's trusting nature react to *this* information?

"Look at the whole system," Cindy had said wisely, "and there is value in having a healthy system, and a healthy system is good for kids." I couldn't agree more, but I winced because the system is not healthy. "When there is trust, people take good risks that are also good for kids." Again, I agreed with Cindy. Again, I cringed. Who can teachers trust?

"I know that I am not a member of a Political Action Committee (PAC), so none of my money goes to politics," she'd said confidently. I appreciated Cindy's commitment to education, but it was clear that she didn't understand how her dues were spent by the union she trusted.

CHAPTER 13

THE FAIR SHARE/
AGENCY FEE PAYER

I have a crinkled manila envelope in my drawer with a canceled stamp date and a broken clasp. It's relabeled in black Sharpie with "union alternatives info." Inside is a magazine called *Teachers in Focus* from October 1999.[97] My parents gave it to me after college, just when I'd become a licensed teacher and was job hunting. We knew that while teaching in Oregon, I'd be required to pay union dues. An article in the Teachers in Focus magazine featuring Barb Amidon, a Washington teacher who objected to her dues being used for politics, let me know I had options.

My first brush with teachers unions came while I was a substitute in Oregon. I was required to fill out a union form. I didn't want to be a member, but I had to sign a form anyway. Was my faith in God large enough to see me through the peer pressure I would experience because of nonmembership?

The peer pressure mounted like gathering storm clouds when the teachers union actively attempted to recruit me after receiving a full-time teaching position in Colorado. When I arrived, I was beyond ecstatic to finally have a classroom of my own. The district had hired a large number of teachers that year and promptly gave us all a stack of books to read for inspiration. They loaded us onto a school bus for a driving tour of the entire district. I thought I'd died and gone to educational heaven, so I didn't even mind that we also had several days of training and meetings.

One meeting in particular stands out in my mind. We were required (or were we invited?) to meet with the local union. It was all a bit fuzzy because most meetings were mandatory for all new hires to the district. Having worked in Oregon as a substitute, I knew a bit about having to pay union dues, so I was listening. They began talking about "having a voice." Suddenly, the group in charge of the meeting was walking around with crisp twenty dollar bills fanned out in their fingers. I woke up! What were they saying? One of them came to our table. A brush of cash was thrust under my nose. Around and around these union members walked, telling us to join. If we joined that day, we could have the cash they were waving under our chins! But after that, our paychecks would take a hit each month, they quietly added. Colorado was a right-to-work state, meaning the payment of dues to a union couldn't be required as a condition of employment. The union had to resort to coercion to gain members.

I was indignant. *So, what if I could have this cash right now? The union was going to get it back later in payroll deductions anyway from anyone who signed on!* I failed to see how union membership would benefit me since I was accountable to parents and teaching in a school district with an Employee Input Process. I was too insulted by the cash tactic and too green to understand it all. They passed out free local education association t-shirts with smiles on their faces, assuring us we could join at any time; however, there would not be a cash bonus if we waited until later to sign up.

Reminiscing on my experience in Colorado reminded me of years later while I worked as a full-time educator in Oregon. Unlike Colorado, Oregon union dues were mandatory. The union storm clouds began to produce angry lightning and thunder as I grimaced at this stipulation. "You may as well join; you have to pay the dues anyway," union officers sing-songed. Government employees in Oregon had to pay union dues as a condition of employment; there was no way out. My money was taken from me.

Collection of dues was a system put in place in the private sector when the National Labor Relations Act of 1935 allowed unions to do so. Originally, employees had a choice to be paying members or not of any labor organization representing their workplace. Then, some individual states decided to require by law that dues be paid as a condition of employment in the public sector, while other states retained a choice for employees in the public sector or "right-to-work" without paying dues.

"You get a voice in education policy. You get legal protection," the union representatives sounded off, almost tauntingly. They knew no one had a choice; they would profit regardless of membership—or nonmembership—

status. "We always provide good snacks at meetings," (It must have been caviar, because dues climbed to over $900 a year.)

I began researching what my rights were in regard to unions since dues were mandatory. While I could not opt out of paying, I could opt out of membership. My first step was pulling out the crinkly manila envelope with the 1999 *Teachers in Focus* magazine. In it, I found information about purchasing professional liability insurance from the Association of American Educators or Christian Educators Association International.[98] I had no need to join the union; I could get my own professional liability coverage.

The next step included asking some questions of my building union representative who had approached me about membership. How is it possible for the union to politically represent over 40,000 Oregon educators who most likely run the gamut of political views? I wanted to know. Her answer was something like this: "We have representatives from each district at state union assemblies. But, if you're not a union member you wouldn't get to go, and you won't get to have your voice heard." I was undaunted; I didn't need a union to make my voice heard on political issues. Every citizen has the right to speak to their elected officials, create petitions, and rally for change.

I was frightened about asking too many questions because I'd heard about the ostracism non-union members could endure from colleagues. A friend and teacher in California had been called names and treated rudely. A culture of fear persisted amongst teachers; no one dared be caught on the "wrong" side of the union. Only a tiny bit of courage existed in me. If I had dug deeply into what is true of me in Christ, I may have been more boldly vocal at that time. Rather than share my misgivings about the union with others, and a desire for different representation, I chose the easy route that brought as little attention to me as possible. I asked the local union co-president if the liability insurance the union offers would be in my name. Her reply was uncertain and took her off guard. I'd learned that the "insurance" the union offers is not in individual teacher's names. What happens if I don't become a member but a fair share fee payer? She said fair share fee payers' money "goes to charity" and I'd be getting a "free ride." (I'm not sure how being *forced to pay dues* was "free," and I already knew that fair share fees *went to the union*.)

Opting out of the political and ideological portion of dues, also known as being an "agency fee payer" or "fair share fee payer" had been an option since 1986 when the U.S. Supreme Court decided on the *Chicago Teachers Union vs. Hudson* case.[99] Why did so few teachers know about this choice? The final decision in *Chicago Teachers Union vs. Hudson* required teachers unions to disclose their fiscal spending and allow teachers to stop paying the portion of dues being spent on political and ideological purposes. Those teachers who decline to pay this portion of dues were known as "agency fee" or "fair share fee" payers.

With all the union training about recruitment, it was odd that the local union officers seemed completely in the dark about the options then available for teachers, specifically the option to be an agency fee payer, and if applicable, a religious objector. This conveniently caused a situation where the misinformation and/or omission of teachers' rights regarding membership and dues payments meant most teachers were backed into a corner and just threw up their hands and joined.

It was common for me to discover teachers didn't understand the concept of "fair share fee payer." Teachers were never informed that agency fee payers were educators who wished to avoid paying for the union's *political and ideological* purposes, but still paid as much as eighty percent of dues. Logically then, any educator paying *full* dues *was* paying for politics, but fair share fee payers (supposedly) were not. Unions had a healthy campaign across the nation of calling educators who chose the fair share fee payer option "free riders" and "scabs" at the *least*. Tactics like what Nathan had experienced—ridicule, targeted personal attacks, and constant pressure—were tools they wielded against teachers to mitigate the number of nonmember agency fee payers.[100]

The differences between membership and nonmembership are few but significant. Nonmembers are not covered under the union's legal protection plan. In most cases, they aren't allowed to vote on the contract, hold office, or attend meetings, leaving them voiceless in regard to their own employment contract. My rights to representation were effectively sabotaged, but of course, nonmembers still had to pay dues. I could relate to the frustrations experienced by the Boston Tea Party colonists long ago who were taxed without representation.

Granted, if you agree with the social justice activism the union espouses, you may not mind mandatory dues. In fact as Ashley, an Oregon teacher, later told me, "I'm happy to make a donation to lobby for education on the local, state, and national level." But forced dues have never been a "donation." They're an infringement on the right to free speech and free association. Neither are dues on parallel with taxes. Taxpayers have voting rights, can be in office themselves, and put initiatives on the ballot. Non-union member teachers forced to pay dues to a union with whom they disagree have no voting rights, can't be in office, and are not allowed to introduce initiatives, yet they had to pay.

I had opted to be an agency fee payer since my political and ideological beliefs were vastly different than the policies that the union lobbied for at all government levels and had pushed the school board to adopt. To take this option, I had to send off a form every year to the union telling them of my decision, along with a few other details. What other club asks you for your home address, telephone number, and *social security number* so you *don't* have to join?

I still had to pay agency fees to the union, which supposedly covered the cost of my *inclusion* in the collective bargaining unit (but I couldn't vote or hold office). The union's insistence on being the exclusive bargainer meant they had to represent all employees in the unit. I wanted the chance to choose who represented me.

After becoming an agency fee payer (rather than a member) in 2012, a packet arrived in the mail. I leaned against my kitchen counter as I opened the envelope, my curiosity growing. What is this? In the envelope I'd just opened, along with a letter from the Oregon Education Association (OEA) begging me to join, were two booklets called a *Hudson Notice*. One detailed dues spending at the state level, and the other was an audited fiscal report of the union's spending at the national level (NEA). Every year you're an agency fee payer, by law, you received this *Hudson Notice.*[101]

In all mandatory union states, you were required to pay full union membership dues or the agency fee mentioned above as a condition of employment. If you were unaware you had the agency fee option, it's because the union didn't want you to know it. They never mentioned it at union orientations and representatives are not trained in how it worked. This acted to boost membership numbers and dues revenue through the deceit of omission. Only *non*members received an audited fiscal report of union spending via the *Hudson Notice.*

Blake, a former agency fee payer in Oregon who'd received the union's *Hudson* fiscal report, described it this way: "When I send in my fair-share opt-out letter, I receive a packet with pages and pages of gibberish," he'd said sardonically. "I get no straightforward, easy-to-read statement of where my money goes," he added. "Dues get taken out of my paycheck and I don't know who gets it or where it gets sent."[102]

For reasons I don't recall now, I showed one of the *Hudson Notice* booklets to the union association representative. She wondered what it was. She wanted a copy. The association representative was also a district union co-president. The union only sent me this audited report because it was required by law. But, there is no law stating they must share detailed fiscal reports with their actual members, which may explain why one of their local presidents had never seen one.

I changed my agency fee payer status to religious objector when it became obvious after continued research that union dues were used to fund Planned Parenthood.[103] As a religious objector, my dues were to be sent to a charity. Aggravatingly, it had to be a charity from a list the union provided, and nonsensically one that wasn't "religious." I knew diverting my dues was the right thing to do. The trouble was, I kept the information to myself out of fear. Other educators have similar beliefs about the sanctity of life and sex education, yet I feared union retribution enough to keep my religious objector standing under wraps. Although Scripture says, "The righteous are as bold as a lion,"[104] I felt more like a cornered kitten.

CHAPTER 14
TEACHERS UNIONS TODAY

Slapping government employees with required payments from their checks to the union was a slick trick of Mr. Wolfe's. His end was to raise cash and his means, the wily use of the legislative process to make legal procurement of dues a condition of employment. "The seventh rule of the ethics of means and ends is that generally success or failure is a mighty determinant of ethics."[105] Taking money straight out of teacher's wallets was "right" and "ethical" for Mr. Wolfe because it served his self-interests. Others be damned, I guess.

Granted, teachers had many positive things to say about the union support they received. They praised their local representatives and negotiating team. It was Gloria, a much beloved and respected (now retired) educator who helped me more deeply understand union representation.[106] She recalled the time when teachers would negotiate with the community for their salaries. The community would vote on the school budget. This could at times become very contentious. Now, most school districts collectively bargain with a union. "It's less obvious in taxes that the community is getting money out of their food budget to pay teachers . . . so there is less contention," she said. This lack of transparency, however, has allowed collective bargaining to be a tool unions use to build power.

When public schools began around the 1850s, communities wanted to pay as little in taxes as possible for public school teachers. Given the chance, they'd shortchange public workers. After all, people generally don't like paying taxes even though they understand the importance of public workers. Some protections are needed, a balance hashed out between the taxpayers and the wages-from-taxes earners. It's safe to say the balance has shifted; taxpayers are at a disadvantage regarding government unions. Yet, teachers and the general public fail to see the power unions wield through the collective bargaining process.

I sought out teachers to converse with whom I knew had different political perspectives and personal beliefs. Barbara fit this description.[107] I wanted to try to see the issue through a different lens. We're friends and I've learned a lot from her over the years. Our friendship is proof you can love, respect, and intelligently discuss issues with someone even when you disagree on a variety of topics.

How would Barbara react to my questions about unions? She and I approach life differently. One of us is conservative, the other progressive. Stereotypes contain grains of truth but are still generalizations. For example, a Democrat may surprise you with their pro-life stance or a Republican with their anti-gun views. Perhaps that is why I was pleasantly surprised to find a friend in Barbara, and she in me, because we could see beyond our stereotypes to engage in respectful conversation and healthy debate.

As a nonmember speaking to a union member, I figured Barbara would be savvy about union dues, member services, and current union topics—in short, she was a more active union member than most. "A lot of [dues money] goes to the local branch and they use that to help with bargaining education and knowing your rights as a teacher," Barbara stated. She knew that some dues went to state but was unsure about national. I was surprised. Barbara was knowledgeable about current events but unsure of dues spending. Did she know about union legal services? Bargaining costs? Other uses of dues? The resolve for my project deepened. Bringing to light truths about union membership might not be met with smiles and acceptance, but I didn't want to see my friends remain in the dark about their union. Or any other teacher for that matter, regardless of their politics, beliefs, or membership status. *Teachers just need to know.*

Fortunately, Barbara did reflect knowledge of the union in other ways. I still had a lot to learn. "Unions educate the community about the school district, what your teachers do," Barbara explained. *Oh yeah, that would be important,* I mused. "The union gives us information on laws that are happening at the state and federal level so we can be aware of things impacting education," she continued. Teachers rely heavily on their union magazine for this. Although not a member, for some reason, the union sent me *Today's OEA* magazines, in which the union reports on blocking and writing legislation. The magazines tell members what the union has decided to do in the legislature and encourages them to support it with letters, phone calls, and capitol steps rallies.

"Any teacher can go to training to understand the contract . . . what the teacher and their employer can and cannot do," Barbara went on. The teachers who sit at the bargaining table for negotiations are trained before bargaining begins, but beyond that, I've never heard about members going to training to understand their contract. I'm sure I'd have heard through the grapevine if union-offered training was taking place, but no such thing ever occurred. I have no way of telling how many teachers actually read their contract, let alone ask questions about it; however, I can infer from my interview samples and significant time spent around teachers that it's very few. "I don't have time to read the whole contract," is the unspoken agreement amongst teachers. "Just give me the nitty-gritty. I'm busy."

Barbara suggested I ask teachers in subsequent interviews about their understanding of the history of unions. She listed the protections we have in place because of the work of unions: "Forty-hour work week, federal holidays, sick pay, family leave . . . half-hour lunch, and periodic breaks . . . The unions helped create a better work environment," Barbara explained. Yes, thank goodness for those people brave enough to come together to push against workplace injustices. Private sector businesses and public institutions don't have a choice on whether or not to comply, and employees have lawful avenues for recourse. "If a company [or school district] provided these things, there would be no need for unions because the employees would be being treated well," Barbara finished. *Oh, if it were that simple.* A little thing called human nature always gets in the way. Unfortunately, there will always be bad bosses, bad employees, poor decisions, and events that could have been prevented at *any* job. Of course, Barbara understands all this. Her valid points enabled me to examine teachers unions from more angles.

The list she gave of union-created worker protections are now *laws*. Are unions no longer needed? If unions went away, what would it be like? Do teachers and the general public believe unions to be a champion force protecting educators? If so, who or what is it that teachers so desperately need protection from?

After meeting with Barbara, I spent time studying and researching the history of teaching. I gained a new appreciation for the work union organizers did in the first half of the twentieth century. Dana Goldstein, author of *The Teacher Wars,* succinctly walks through the history of the teaching profession in America.[108] It has always been embattled by the ebb and flow of whatever national debate or calamity is occurring. The origination of unions have served a purpose; they accomplished for workers what needed to be done. The historical reasons for unions are just that—history. We're in a new point on the timeline.

Teachers are expected to carry the weight of responsibility for the nation's success. We are wearied by burdensome expectations, beloved yet blamed. We shoulder the clamor surrounding education while soldiering on inside our classrooms. This is my perspective from the twenty-first century, when I don't have to battle against men's attitudes that women are inferior, unfair pay, and squalid school buildings, thanks to those who fought for better conditions long ago.

I came to understand that most teachers want to have a union. The local union settles grievances, handles negotiations, and provides teachers with support. Disaffiliation with state and national unions would allow local-only unions to blossom. Teachers would pay less dues, retain protections, and enjoy truly autonomous decision-making centered on the needs of the community at hand. No state or national union would be setting policies, demanding action, or making decisions from far away. The historically recognized need for management and employees to come to mutual agreement about working conditions via a union would remain intact, while the power-hungry and politically motivated elements would drop away. Current teachers would have the opportunity to use what's always existed but has been suppressed for years by elite unions: the right to regularly vote on who represents us.

At this point in time, state and national unions have expropriated control of school policy from the hands of both parents and teachers. Lax discipline, Common Core, and inappropriate sex education lessons are *not* in place because parents and teachers wanted them. Unions control the system and maneuver those within it to achieve union ends. Parents and teachers want what is best for students and their community. State and national unions want *control* of students and communities. Teachers unions must be understood for what they are right *now*, in the twenty-first century.

CHAPTER 15

TRACKING DUES

According to the September 2017 *Hudson Notice*, the nonprofit NEA collected $362,188,445 in 501(c)(5) nonprofit-status tax-exempt dues.[109] This is merely the *national level* dues collected. My jaw hit the floor when I learned what happens to some of the money gathered through teacher union dues at the state and national level: soft money donations and political action committees (PACs). Soft money donations are monies given in faith that they'll be used for the stated purpose, but then the recipient diverts them elsewhere. To illustrate, let's say you decide to donate money to your local food bank. You fully trust and expect the money to be used to feed those who are hungry. Instead, the food bank turns around and gives your money to the local library campaign. Both are worthwhile causes, but you spoke up for hungry people, not building a library. Organizations that wish to influence politics by financially supporting various candidate campaigns or ballot measures form PACs.

You can find possible soft money use of dues through partnerships explained in union publications such as this:

"The Oregon Education Association and Family Forward Action have joined together with Planned Parenthood Advocates of Oregon, Oregon AFL-CIO, AFSCME . . ." from the fall 2014 *Today's OEA* magazine.[110]

The Council of Chief State School Officers is an example of a soft money diversion of teachers' dues. This group was involved in placing the Common Core standards, via "Race to the Top", in nearly all states. It is a nonprofit, private organization. Did union members approve supporting this group with dues?

The Economic Policy Institute is another odd redirection of dues money.[111] This nonprofit organization states that its goal is to help low- and middle-income workers through research and application of economic policies. The NEA is listed as a donor in the "$200,000 and up" category.[112] Seven of the people on its board are presidents of labor organizations, including the NEA and AFT presidents. What does this organization have to do with *teacher* advocacy?

My research also led me to an article by David Schmus, president of Christian Educators Association International. In it he explains, "I found that almost $800,000 found its way from the National Education Association (NEA) to Planned Parenthood during the 2014 election cycle." A later 2016 article of his traces yet another NEA contribution to Planned Parenthood.[113] Why are unions donating dues to controversial causes in the first place? Their money is supposed to be used to support the nation's teachers.

Consider the portion of dues that are sent to Education

International, a confederation of teachers unions from around the world. According to the website unionfacts.com, $10,000 was sent from NEA to Education International (EI) in 2015.[114] Mary Futrell, former NEA president, was once president of Education International, according to Lois Weiner's book, *The Future of Our Schools.*[115] Weiner describes herself as a lifelong teacher union activist, and at the time of the book's publication, was a New Jersey City University Professor. She discloses in her book that getting more U.S. teachers involved with the international union contingent should be an "organizing priority" and that adding more U.S. participants "can add resources and political contacts that can benefit Latin American unions." Why would United States teachers want to send more money from their paychecks to unknown recipients in foreign countries?

Teachers' dues also fund PACs, even if teachers don't voluntarily choose this option. For example, an organization called Defend Oregon received union money. Their website claims, "Extremist groups with dangerous agendas are setting their sights on Oregon."[116] Defend Oregon, in general, actively blocks any conservative efforts in the state and happily accepts donations from the OEA. Defend Oregon supported measure Measure 91 which—in 2014— was put to voters regarding the legalization of recreational marijuana.

"[I]n 2014 the teacher union Oregon Education Association (OEA) contributed $700,000 to Defend

Oregon PAC, then Defend Oregon contributed $300,000 to the Yes on 91 PAC. Ballot measure 91 subsequently passed and legalized the recreational use of marijuana in Oregon. There is no rational public policy reason for a teacher union to support the recreational use of a federally banned substance. Moreover, this issue has nothing to do with a legitimate collective bargaining topic," states an amicus brief in *Friedrichs vs. California Teachers Association*, a case defending free speech and association.[117]

The AFT and the NEA are registered with the Internal Revenue Service (IRS) as 501(c)(5) nonprofit organizations and are affiliated with state and local level unions—501(c)(5) nonprofits cannot directly contribute to candidates. They can and do support candidates *indirectly* with items such as signs and advertisements. The Center for Responsive Politics describes 501(c)s: "These are nonprofit, tax-exempt groups organized under section 501(c) of the Internal Revenue Code. These groups can engage in varying amounts of political activity. And because they are not technically political organizations, they are not required to disclose their donors to the public."[118] In 2016, the AFT was the largest 527 contributor at $17,598,449, given entirely to support the causes of Democrats[119] (527 refers to the tax code that regulates an organization's contributions toward actions impacting elections and policy issues at the local, state and federal level). So, when my colleague Cindy said she intentionally opted out of a voluntary donation to her union PAC, she was unaware a portion of her dues are given to PACs of the union's choosing anyway.

Kira, a dedicated elementary school teacher working in a small town in North Carolina, knew more about teachers unions than most teachers I spoke with, readily stating knowledge about dues going to the local, state, and national level. She spoke tenderly of her students, and animatedly shared some of their recent progress in lessons. She was aware of unions' wealth, and how some of it is used for wining and dining legislators: "I mean, I don't know . . . but I would think that it is very hard to take a congressman out to dinner and you know, take him to Wendy's."[120]

"I don't believe my money should go to political interests that I oppose," said Judy, an educator who'd taught at the elementary level for more than 30 years prior to becoming a principal. "I should be able to decide if that is what I want to do as opposed to just paying and not knowing where the money is going."[121]

Just as Judy was not informed about how her dues were spent, teachers in New Jersey were clueless about how their dues were being spent during a 2017 state senate election. Leah Mishkin of New Jersey Television News (NJTV) interviewed teachers at a conference just before the campaign.[122] Their answers, caught on video, exposed their ignorance of the union's use of dues.

"Those millions of dollars are voluntary donations by members, called PAC [political action committee] donations. So, it's not like it's money that comes out of dues dollars. So, I'm perfectly fine," said NJEA member Robert Scardino.

Another NJEA member, Barbara Toczko, said, "All the money that went to support our candidates along the way . . . it was PAC money. It differs because it's not dues money . . . Dues goes for everything else but it doesn't go for political."

In truth, the NJEA spent $4.5 million on promoting a candidate and $5.7 million total in the general election. Once again, a union had been successful in deluding its members into thinking money for politics comes only from *voluntary* PAC donations. The union itself explains in the *Hudson Notice* (the audited financial report) the calculations of the *portion of regular dues* that are used for *political and ideological* purposes.

At the event in New Jersey, NJEA president Marie Blistan stated, "We exist from member's dues, and again for the purpose of advocating on behalf of them . . . We absolutely use some of our money to promote those causes, because as you know in public education, everything is either legislative, it's regulated, or it's by statute."

NJTV was able to prove through the Election Law Enforcement Commission that the NJEA had founded a 527 PAC called Garden State Forward and channeled funds through that for political purposes. Furthermore, they received confirmation via email from NJEA communications director Steve Baker that the $5.7 million came from membership dues *not* voluntary PAC donations.[123]

Teachers are trusting their unions to provide legal protection and collective bargaining services. However, large portions of their money are being diverted to political and ideological purposes they may not support or that have nothing to do with education. Educators ought to refuse to let the union rob their political and ideological free speech and association through diversion of their hard-earned money.

The political uses of dues weren't the only concern I had.

Most employees working for the state and national unions receive six-figure total compensation packages. For example, AFT president Randi Weingarten makes about $472,197 per year[124] and former NEA president Lily Eskelsen-Garcia's was paid approximately $396,616 per year.[125] Contrast that with the fact teachers are all paid similarly from the same tired salary schedule. Few opportunities for increased pay through leadership, excellent performance and results, specialized talent, or differing workloads exist. Wouldn't we rather be rewarded when we step up to make our instruction first-class than to bear the weight of six-figure incomes paid to union executives?

Insights from Gloria, the retired teacher and administrator who helped me understand the role of unions, came to mind. "I was most disgusted both as a teacher and as an administrator—teachers are taking a cut because we had to cut days and the union didn't give teachers a break," she explained. "They still expected the same work. What kind of love from the union is this for the people you are taking care of? Especially when I found out the secretaries in the union made more than my teachers. Not that I don't think secretaries aren't worth it, but if your secretaries are making that, then why aren't the unions fighting for better incomes for their teachers? I have no idea what union leaders make. If the secretaries make more than a teacher, then I can imagine!"[126]

Along with dues, the union receives corporate sponsorships and makes business decisions as if it were a corporate entity.[127] Part of NEA's recruitment package includes discount coupons and services. These are delivered through the NEA Member Benefit Corporation.[128] The NEA Member Benefit Corporation is a wholly owned subsidiary of the NEA.[129] Another source of revenue for teachers unions was rental property income of $1,565,110 in 2015 from NEA Property, *Incorporated*.[130] Yet, in a volume of the union's magazine, *Today's OEA*, the union complains about corporations funding a ballot measure they despised, stating further that "Corporate profits are off the charts."[131] The NEA's own coffers are quite full, yet teachers are led to believe their union is anti-corporation and anti-profit.

Granted, any organization that has a message to advance and goals to achieve will need funding, perhaps through corporate sponsorship. It isn't wrong to find funding for the goals you have. The teachers unions regularly accept grants and financial support from foundations and the like, as do other organizations with visions for education reform. Nonetheless, teachers and taxpayers don't—for the most part—understand the enormous wealth the teachers unions possess nor are they informed of how union dues are utilized. Teachers' money in the form of union dues from NEA's and AFT's national, state, and local affiliates rolls in at over $1 billion every year.[132]

When I asked teachers across the country if they'd ever seen a union fiscal report, no one had. Heather, a union representative and teacher from Utah, responded this way: "I know they have it. I have never actually seen a copy of it. If I asked for it, they would show me a copy."[133] Ashley, a fifteen-year veteran teacher admitted, "No, not to my knowledge. The treasurers give reports at meetings. I would check the website. It could be online or in the contract."[134] How have teachers come to this place of blind trust in their union and ignorance about what their own contracts contain?

The present state and national unions are a dominating political and cultural force. Former NEA President Lily Eskelsen Garcia suggested, in reference to the Democratic Party's 2016 platform on education, that the NEA may have written it. In fact, she told *Education Week:* "I think we actually kind of did."[135]

What I was learning about unions was weighing heavier and heavier upon me. "The act of faith is what becomes a shield of protection," Priscilla Shirer wrote in her book *The Armor of God.*[136] I had to trust and *act like* He would continue to protect me, not just from physical harm, but also the weight of knowing so many heavy things about an organization my dear colleagues trust.

CHAPTER 16

LUCK OF THE CONTRACT-HIRING-ORDER DRAW

My stomach was disrupted by butterflies a few years ago when I sat with my brother, also a teacher, hoping his number wouldn't be drawn first. For all new hires, the district determined "seniority" by luck of the draw. Each year, new hires all had the same hire date, and since the union contract dictated a last-in, first-out policy, the district had to determine some sort of order. Unions might blame this on the district; however, it's the *union's* demand that teachers be retained or let go based on hiring order rather than on merit and performance.

"The reality is that many teachers do not benefit from union representation; some are even clearly disadvantaged by it. For example, some teachers who lose their jobs when there is a reduction in force (RIF) would be retained if not for a union contract that requires the district to make layoffs in reverse order of seniority," Myron Lieberman states succinctly in his book *Understanding the Teacher Union Contract*.[137]

Not only can good teachers be let go, but bad teachers can be hard to fire. "Even though the union is a powerful strength and support for a teacher, it also has a negative flip side where it is also hard to get rid of an ineffective teacher. I have given this thought before. I've lived it and seen it. This is where the union is a double-edged sword," mused Susan, the Oregon elementary teacher whom I'd met with just before the start of a new school year. I wanted to know more about the situation she was alluding to, but she was already generously carving out so much time for me. Susan is a gem; a teacher who pours out her heart helping students and their parents alongside devoting time to colleagues.[138]

Seniority and tenure written into contracts means teachers may be relegated to working with colleagues who are less than capable at their jobs. Michelle, an educator from Pennsylvania, said, "Even when you are in your own classroom, you work collaboratively. If someone else is not pulling their own weight, it drags the morale of the team down and makes it challenging. Communication and the team start to fall apart. If one person is not performing, it really does affect everyone."[139] The frustration she felt with these types of situations came through in her voice.

Em, a high school teacher from Kansas, made clear how important quality teacher evaluation is and how understanding student needs is a critical piece to that. "Maybe just getting a student to show up could be a success," she says. "I also want the freshman teacher to be good, because I teach sophomores and it will affect me and what I can do with students. If the teacher is not doing well or making effort to improve, then the students shouldn't have to suffer for that."[140] She knew the students' perspective had to be considered.

Nancy, of Oregon, put it this way: "I think the teacher should be given the opportunity to have more training if they are willing and have support from the principal. The key is the teacher has to be willing to continue to grow."[141] It would be hard to find any teacher who didn't feel their colleagues deserve the chance to improve and master the art of teaching. It would also be hard to find any teacher who wanted to continue working with a colleague who never lifted a finger and mistreated or neglected students.

"Teachers shouldn't stay in teaching just to stay or be there if they are performing poorly. If you are not performing in other jobs, you don't get a raise, or you just don't keep the job. Unfortunately, we don't run education like that," said Nicole, an elementary school teacher from Oregon.[142] Most teachers "race" to excellence year after year, striving to bring about a win for each child in their classroom like a race car driver seeking a trophy. Unlike car racing, however, teachers who lag behind are allowed to stay on the track.

As administrators like Gloria know, "It's like the occasional bad teacher colors the reputation of the good teachers, like a bad cop flavors the reputation of the good cops. The union got in the way of us helping teachers or getting teachers out of there who were bad teachers. There are just some people who aren't good teachers." She'd often run into union roadblocks when she had teachers who really should have been let go. "The union often got in the way of the plan to improve. For example, making restrictions of the plan so difficult that there was really no way the teacher would improve. When I was going into administrative work it was beaten into us that a plan of improvement is a plan for improvement, not just a plan to get rid of somebody."[143]

As I sat in the room with my brother witnessing the "seniority" number draw, I wanted to yell at the administrators, union members, and teachers there with us: "Why do you let this go on?" It's as though no one is allowed to recognize excellent, effective teaching. Why work hard? Could my brother's self-motivation and love for students keep him in this devastatingly difficult job?

I was astonished to come across a similar criticism from a former president of the AFT, Albert Shanker: "It's time to admit that public education operates like a planned economy, a bureaucratic system in which everybody's role is spelled out in advance and there are few incentives for innovation and productivity. It's no surprise that our school system doesn't improve: It more resembles the communist economy than our own market economy."[144]

My brother and I heaved a huge sigh of relief as quietly as we could when his drawn number was "middle of the pack." However, we both knew if layoffs came, he'd only keep his job because of the luck of the draw. It wouldn't matter if he was dedicated to his students and delivering excellent instruction, and it wouldn't matter if other teachers who'd also drawn middle numbers may not be. Under the union contract, neither my brother nor I, beginner or tenured, would ever experience the accolades, advancement opportunities, or financial bonuses for a job well done.

CHAPTER 17

EXCLUSIVE SALARY AND CONTROLLED CORRESPONDENCE

Over the years I've had the privilege of working side-by-side with teachers brand new to the profession. They always bring a zest and enthusiasm that reenergizes me. I watch them strain under the heavy load of being a first-year teacher. Many of them do smashingly well and make the rest of the staff proud to have them on board. It was while witnessing my brother go through this first-year proving ground that I gave more thought to pay discrepancy between new teachers and experienced teachers, as well as the control unions exert over communication that keeps teachers intentionally *un*informed.

When you start out in teaching, you step onto a pay ladder that increases your income based on each year you work and professional development coursework credits. We work in a highly dynamic, intense profession that requires a wide range of skills and comes with the awesome weight of impacting a child's future. Yet everyone, regardless of skill, effort, or workload, gets paid according to the same formula. Unfortunately, this system "discourages high-

quality people from entering teaching (and staying), because
. . . unlike in a truly professional setting, their talent and
success will not get rewarded," explains Terry Moe in his
book *Special Interest*.[145]

Why should my hard-working brother, or any other
hard-working beginning teacher, be paid based *solely* on
their years of experience and schooling? I'd witnessed
amazingly talented beginning teachers being paid less
than $40,000 and shouldering the same job expectations
as far less talented teachers who'd been teaching for years
and years. Since the contract stipulated pay according
to a salary schedule, which was devoid of any caveat for
excellent performance, some of the best teachers were
laboring for peanuts. With my brother now teaching, this
oversight rankled me. I wanted changes, but of course, the
union wanted to maintain control of salaries rather than
acknowledge excellence in teaching; that would threaten
their power structure.

For example, the New Mexico teachers unions blatantly
opposed teachers receiving bonuses in a new program the
governor approved in March 2018. The teachers unions,
who constantly chatter about increasing teacher pay,
attempted to block the bonuses. "This week, Gov. [sic]
Susana Martinez signed off on a budget bill that provides
for $5,000 and $10,000 bonuses for exemplary teachers in
New Mexico," stated the *Albuquerque Journal*. "[O]ne union
leader says her group might still be able to block the bonuses
by invoking their collective bargaining rights under state

law." *Is the teachers union for or against teachers?* I wondered. The *Journal's* editor-written article concluded with, "It's not unusual for NEA and AFT to draw a line in the sand—but it's a sad day when they are willing to stand in the way of deserving teachers receiving . . . bonuses."[146]

Most teachers, after several years on the job, enjoy decent total compensation packages. Health insurance, retirement accounts, and plenty of time off are welcome benefits for dedicated, hard-working individuals. If this compensation were based on the effort and excellence of job performance, teacher morale would rise. If teachers could, after gaining years of experience in one district, make a lateral move for similar pay and benefits in another district, that would be a system improvement. As it stands now, teachers with talent, experience and quality references take severe pay cuts if they choose to change districts. Once again, the union-negotiated salary schedules and agreements put teachers between a rock and a hard place.

Typical contracts don't respect variances in workload, either. A longtime community college professor, Mary, made this very clear.[147] She's seen many changes come and go. Leaning on the kitchen counter and speaking earnestly, Mary shared her thoughts on workload at the community college level. "It's really different to me as a nursing instructor to go in and teach what they call a clinical lab in the hospital that required hours and hours of prep versus supervising a chemistry lab that used the same equipment and setting day after day. That was what the argument was always about: equity of workload."

Michael and Gloria, teachers who'd worked together in a small-town school district for over a decade, gave me insight on how contract rules debilitated the efforts of a hard-working teacher who was seeking to do right by her students.

"When I was teaching, the primary kids would be bussed home at 2 p.m., and the intermediates would be bussed home at 3 p.m. I had a 2/3 blend, so in December I offered the second graders the option to stay for that last hour, until 3 p.m. That extra hour made such a difference!" Gloria recalled with pride. Students received more instruction and practice time with concepts. "The union stepped in and said having different teacher hours wasn't equitable," she relayed with lament.[148] Rather than recognize the benefit students were receiving and the willingness of teachers to put in the extra effort, the union shortened the school day for all grade levels. If you're truly advocating for teachers, you'd support their innovative and student-centered ideas, not undermine them. Why must salaried professionals work the exact same hours, anyway? It appears that individuality and ingenuity threaten the unions.

According to Michael, this issue was swirling in their district along with a threat to strike over salary and these "inequitable" working conditions. "At the elementary school, we were working about an hour and ten minutes longer for kindergarten through third grade kids, and about half an hour longer for fourth and fifth grade kids," he said.[149] Obviously, the teachers who'd chosen to have their students longer into the afternoon were bitter about the attitude some coworkers adopted toward the situation. Had providing students with more instruction really needed to become a grievance brought by a few teachers over "inequity"? Or was it a case of Mr. Wolfe purposely churning up issues as a means to keep the organization buzzing with action? After all, he believes constant friction and having "issues" to resolve are essential to an organization's survival—those issues are its oxygen.[150]

Students at different ages need different types and amounts of support from their teachers. Contracts demanding strict adherence to every teacher working exactly the same minutes—in exactly the same time frames and schedules—squeeze out the very real differences and needs between grade levels. What's more important— exacting equity for all teachers—or kids receiving what they need? Certainly, many teachers work hours outside their contract requirements, but in some districts, this is vigorously frowned upon in a union effort to promote uniformity. Unions laud teacher equity to the detriment of teacher autonomy and professional decision-making, not to mention students' needs. In any other field, salaried professionals, by definition, work varied hours and flex to deliver quality and excellence. In education, professionalism is stifled, and students shortchanged when "equity" rules the contract.

"The truth is performance pay threatens the teachers unions' monopoly over their members. Thus, teachers must be indiscriminately lumped together, their pay must be the same, and any teacher, no matter how good, who voices any dissent or does any extra work beyond the minimum outlined by contract, must be punished,"[151] said Rod Paige, former U.S. Secretary of Education.

If a school district were to base pay on not just years of experience but also skill and performance, providing opportunities where I could earn bonuses or move into leadership positions for top pay, I would want to work there. I would feel valued, noticed, and quite *professional*.

Michelle Rhee, former chancellor of schools in D.C., garnered widespread attention when she offered teachers the unusual opportunity to make six-figure salaries! Can you believe the teachers *turned it down?*[152] The D.C. teachers were inundated with messages the union sends to all educators: "Teachers shouldn't compete with each other. It's impossible to quantify good teaching. Management would play favorites. The benefit to students is not proven."[153] These unions that claim to be fighting for teacher salaries convinced teachers *to turn down* the chance to earn six-figure salaries. All the while, state and national union leaders were taking home six-figure salaries for themselves.

The union says it's fighting to increase teacher pay and vilifies corporations for making profits and not paying what *it* considers high enough taxes. The union constantly repeats there's "not enough education funding" from taxes, even immediately after scoring huge revenue streams from new tax schemes. Yet unions themselves are tax-exempt nonprofit entities. They vehemently oppose charter schools, private schools, home schools, and vouchers—non-public education opportunities that are not bound to union contracts (with a few exceptions) and don't include teachers who pay union dues. Public school teachers have given state and national unions enough dues over the years to put elite union officers at the top of the dog pile. From there they can say anything they wish, while teachers at the bottom are squashed, muted, and essentially told: "The union is speaking on our behalf . . . just keep sending your money."

Despite the issue with teacher pay, current educators have respectable workplaces compared to teachers' working conditions in the late 1800s. Few would deny drastic changes were needed more than a century ago. For example, teachers at the high school level were paid more than those at the elementary level. Schools were often overcrowded. Female teachers were pressing back against the notion that too much intellectual focus would be detrimental to their health. They were expected to be role models of deportment and impart social skills over academic ones. Furthermore, tension and conflicts of interest existed between parents, teachers, and the business community as schools transformed from localized operation to centralization. What qualifications should a teacher have? Who will evaluate teachers? Which curriculum will be used? What portion of taxes should pay salaries, and what portion ought to pay for school construction?[154]

We can all be thankful teachers at that time had the wherewithal to stand up and protest unacceptable conditions. Their work, along with the push of private sector labor unions, brought needed improvements for employees across the nation. The National Labor Relations Act of 1935 was perhaps the catalyst for other policies and laws to be enacted on behalf of workers. We now enjoy several federal laws and agencies that protect all workers: Workers Compensation Laws (early 1900s), Equal Pay Act (1963), Civil Rights Act (1964), Occupational Safety and Health Administration (est. 1970), Family and Medical Leave Act (1993)—*along with* the Constitution of the United States' protections for each and every citizen. Regardless of whether you're part of a labor union or not, you're guaranteed freedom of speech, religion, assembly, and due process.

Would the reality of these laws and existence of rights-guaranteeing founding documents comfort my brother or other low-paid, talented beginning teachers? I wondered how my idealistic perception of a teaching career at the turn of the twenty-first century compared to current beginning teachers' perceptions. The union literature and messages sent to educators impacts their understanding of their role as teachers and of their unions.

In most cases, unions stipulate *they alone* be allowed to put literature in teachers' school mailboxes, post information on bulletin boards, use the district email system for union business, and hold meetings in school buildings. According to your contract, no other educational associations are allowed to do such things.

It's true that unions have exclusive bargaining rights by law, but this law doesn't extend to exclusively being able to *communicate* with teachers—unless, of course, the school board signs a contract giving unions exclusive rights to communicate with teachers. Unions easily persuade school boards into accepting such exclusivity because school boards don't think through the implications. In effect, what happens is educators "lose the opportunity to get information that the union wishes to conceal from the teachers," wrote Myron Lieberman in his book, *Understanding the Teacher Union Contract*.[155] So, news about introduced legislation, such as laws to circumvent the restored freedoms of the *Janus* case (which changed union membership and dues to voluntary rather than mandatory) never gets to teachers unless they know to seek it out. Teacher contracts containing exclusive union communication clauses step on the toes of teachers' freedom to access what the ruling means for them. "Granting a union exclusivity infringes on the rights of individual teachers," Lieberman states.

Perhaps this is why teachers don't realize they have the right to vote for who their exclusive bargainer is. Teachers operate without realizing the union is *not* their permanent representative. Teachers can change their exclusive bargainer when and if thirty percent of unit members vote for such a change, then vote in new representation with a fifty-one percent majority vote. State laws dictate the process, which involves specific steps and must be carefully followed.[156] One benefit of switching exclusive bargainers is that it includes the ability to determine whether your union will be affiliated with the state and national unions. "[I]f people feel they don't have power to change a bad situation, *then they do not think about it*," Mr. Wolfe notes.[157] Worse still is teachers don't realize they're in a bad situation to begin with.

---------------- CHAPTER 18 ----------------
WE'RE HERE TO REPRESENT!

A random memory swirled to my mind. There I was, feet braced, brandishing a wooden-handled mallet, the thick foam head encased in cheap green vinyl. Any minute now I would smack down chomping plastic alligator heads springing up from a cheesy painted pond. My journey to explore and the operation of teachers unions felt a lot like that "whack-a-mole" game.

Access to information from other educational associations? Whack! The bulletin boards, teacher mailboxes, and district email are only for the union. Think the incompetent colleague next door is harming children? Whack! Just give them some time, they'll be tenured, and you'll be stuck with them. Don't like your salary? Whack! All teachers are the same, and we can't tell who's doing a good job anyway. Assume a union lawyer or UniServ representative is present at all collective bargaining negotiations? Whack! This is not true in all instances. Have a grievance? Whack! Never mind your day in court, you'll settle this with binding arbitration.

I spoke with my dad about one of his experiences on the local school board, which included negotiation of teacher contracts. "Once, during negotiations, the union Uniserv representative would . . . [a]t times . . . get up and storm out like that was the end; he was going home," my dad recollected. "[A]fter two or three times . . . I decided to follow him . . . It so happens he was addicted to nicotine." Uniserv representatives are union field employees whose primary jobs are recruiting, organizing, lobbying, and sometimes being around for negotiations. My dad said the reasons for the Uniserv representative to get up were irrational, and not aligned with the predetermined breaks. As soon as Dad found out it was all about needing a smoke break, his sentiment was, "He was getting paid a lot of money for not doing much."[158] Currently, Uniserv representatives make six-figure salaries plus benefits.

Uniserv representatives are rarely lawyers and aren't always needed during negotiations. If teachers are at the table doing the hard work of negotiations and have been trained in the bargaining process, why not increase *their* stipends and negate the expense of a Uniserv representative? Uniserv representatives are part of state-level union affiliates. They are a large and influential group of "organizers" who are spread out across the nation, recruiting school employees within their assigned region.

Most likely it was a Uniserv representative who spoke to Anna and her coworkers that frightening day when they felt intimidated and pressed to say bad things about their district. "Let us examine what this labor organizer has done. He has taken a group of apathetic workers; he has fanned their resentments and hostilities by a number of means," Mr. Wolfe may brag about Uniserv representatives.[159] These "reps" provide professional development on such topics as equity and bargaining, giving advice to local unions as needed regarding grievance issues; however, these are secondary to pursuit of political action, recruitment, and mobilization of members. "[A] national popular power force cannot come without many organizers," Mr. Wolfe assures.[160] Since Uniserv representatives—who are not lawyers—are particularly focused on organizing and lobbying, it would be more helpful for teachers to have a lawyer on retainer.

Jerry, the retired teacher-turned-lawyer, believes it would benefit teachers and make financial sense for unions to provide a lawyer on retainer to teachers within a bargaining unit.[161] Teachers would have a legal expert as an advocate to address grievances. Lawyers do not appear when teachers have grievances; a fellow association representative teacher from the union accompanies them. I spoke with Jerry over the phone. His voice was confident and exposed some deep, steadfast joy.

"Now think about this: a teacher is going in against the administration to defend himself. What incentive does the teacher have to go to the mat for the teacher who's been called in? Absolutely no incentive. In fact, it's probably to the [union association representative] teacher's benefit to go along with whatever the administration wants to do regardless of how detrimental it may be to the professional standing of the defending teacher," Jerry explained. "If a teacher has been called in for an administrative hearing, that teacher should be able to call up the union and say, 'Can you send an attorney over to accompany me?' And they should do it. Right on the spot!" Jerry said emphatically. Even though teachers are paying hundreds of dollars in dues, no lawyer is on retainer. A coworker, usually the union association representative, goes with the accused teacher to face the administration and address the grievance. Not even a Uniserv representative shows up.

As union activist Lois Weiner points out in her book, *The Future of Our Schools,* "Members have the right to ask that a grievance be filed on their behalf, but in most unions members do not have the right to demand that the matter be pursued in court or in arbitration."[162] This is not the legal representation for which teachers signed up.

Sometimes, as I worked to reveal the connections of people, policies, and money in public education—like a miner after gold—I would drop my tools and weep. Tunnel after tunnel led me to deeper understanding of how the teachers unions operated. I was uncovering nothing but bad news.

If having no right to demand your issue be brought to court or arbitration is not enough of a slap in the face, consider that even *filing* a grievance might be a rough ride. Do you think many New York teachers read their contract? It's 237 pages long![163] Los Angeles's is 408 pages long.[164] Chicago's, 456 pages.[165] The sheer volume of pages would scare me away. If you've been wronged in your work, should it be a hassle just to figure out how to file a grievance? Thankfully, the first step is usually an informal talk with your principal. If that results in no change, you state the problem in writing, being sure to reference the specific contract or policy you feel has been violated. (An arduous task if your contract exceeds the number of pages in your favorite novel.) Next, go over the written grievance in a meeting with your union association representative and your supervisor.

This fellow coworker (association representative) will attempt to help you navigate the process on their own time, sometimes without a stipend from the union for their efforts. Your association representative colleague also has to keep in mind they'll be evaluated by the very administrator to whom you're presenting your grievance. Who do you think would fight harder for you: a caring, unpaid, short-on-time coworker, or a paid lawyer on retainer?

The union talks big about "being there" for teachers should problems arise. Judy, an Oregon teacher, did receive some help from her local representation once but then, "The union couldn't help me because of the nature of the situation."[166] Can the union be trusted to help you or not?

--------- CHAPTER 19 ---------
THE LEGAL PROTECTION
MIRAGE

I experienced trust falls for the first time at summer camp when I was fourteen. A group of fellow campers and our counselor were gathered outside under tall Douglas fir trees. Of course, the coolest and swankiest kid went first. If we could catch him, we could catch anybody. And we did catch him. And the next person, and the next. Much to my relief, the group even caught me.

In trust falls, the one falling hollers out, "Ready?" to the catchers and waits for their reply, "Ready!" before leaning back in faith. Insurance functions like a trust fall in many respects. Albeit the person falling back on the insurance coverage doesn't do it willfully, but because of circumstances beyond their control. The insurer, promising to help in time of need says, "Ready!" And then presumably catches the "faller"—the insured. At camp, I knew the people who'd promised to catch me. Do you know who has promised to "catch" you if an incident occurs while teaching for which you are accused of wrongdoing? Would you be ready to just lean back?

I was sitting at an after-church potluck in North Carolina, everyone helping polish off Thanksgiving leftovers. A retired Virginia teacher, Arnold, and his wife, also a retired teacher, sat to my left. I'd known them barely ten minutes when we plunged into an animated discussion about teachers unions' supposed legal protection. Arnold's assigned union lawyer had never won a case; Arnold eventually had to hire his own personal lawyer, paying out of pocket. "Union membership is a firm grasp on an empty bag!" he nearly yelled. I so badly wanted to hear the whole story, but part of his court agreement was nondisclosure. All I learned was that the union was at fault and hadn't provided him with legal help in his time of need.

Later I learned of another legal situation with a high school teacher, Joel, from Washington, who'd been falsely accused of harming a high school girl. Even after the incident had been reported to his union, they did nothing to stand by him. The accusations were clearly fabrications made up by two students. Still, the union was silent as Joel's administration ordered him to take anger management classes and undergo a psychological examination.

How nice it sounds when the NEA says, "Educators Employment Liability (EEL) insurance policy is just one of many benefits of membership provided at no additional cost to the member."[167] Or a state affiliate says, "As a member, you are covered by this EEL Program policy at no cost to you." No cost? You *pay* dues.

Except, they weren't there for Arnold or Joel.

"It's one of the advertisements. The NEA provides you legal services to help if you need it," Jerry, retired teacher and practicing lawyer, commented. "But the NEA will only provide union help for teachers if doing so advances the NEA's core objectives. You know, to make itself look better and convince teachers that they have to have NEA protection to shield themselves from the evils of . . . being a teacher."[168]

By law, as an employee of a public entity, your employer is bound to provide you with liability insurance as part of the coverage they *must have* for *all* of their employees. These laws are known as *hold harmless laws.* They acknowledge there's a risk involved in providing certain services because of the nature of the job, and provide protections for employers. For a school district, "hold harmless" insurance is protection against incidents arising from day-to-day operations.

"The NEA believes it is the responsibility of your employer to provide you with insurance to protect you from personal financial liability stemming from employment-related lawsuits. NEA supports state 'hold harmless' legislation *which requires that the employer pay for your defense or related damages in case you are sued* [emphasis mine]."[169]

For example, accidental injury to a student is covered in the district's risk management "umbrella" insurance plan and supported with state law. Your union liability insurance coverage will only begin when and if the school district coverage runs out. Basically, if an incident is in the category of coverage under the district's umbrella plan, the union would expect the district to cover any legal expenses. According to the NEA website, "The EEL [Educators Employment Liability] policy covers criminal and civil rights cases, but not cases arising out of the discharge or layoff of a member, or involving other 'job rights' issues . . . These types of cases are covered by the Kate Frank-DuShane Unified Legal Services Program. This policy pays its benefits when other sources of insurance (e.g., a school district professional liability policy) are exhausted."[170]

Kira, a current North Carolina teacher, put it this way: "I really did believe that I needed to be part of the union for the legal protection." At one point, she realized her district already offered her protection against accusations. "If I ever got taken to court or if I was sued by a parent, then my district has a legal team; my district is going to support me."[171]

Kira's statement got me thinking about how the union's admonishments to have legal protection against "issues" had influenced me. Did I sign up for my professional liability insurance from the nonunion American Association of Educators out of fears the *union* had actually perpetuated?

"I've seen the district use their own lawyers to help support teachers," Shelby, a Colorado teacher, added.[172] "Whether or not those teachers were in the union, they have supported teachers with legal action because that's the right thing to do, whether there's a union involved or not."

Arnold and Joel still needed legal assistance, in spite of the school district-provided employee liability insurance required by hold harmless laws. The union failed to protect them. Arnold had to hire his own attorney. Joel had purchased a professional liability insurance plan through Association of American Educators (AAE). AAE provides educators with a policy in the educator's name with wider, better coverage than what the NEA and AFT offer. Joel didn't have a union association representative show up; he had a personal lawyer from AAE. Needless to say, Joel did not attend anger management classes nor have a psychological evaluation. The district administration immediately drew back when Joel's lawyer arrived, and he was restored to the good standing he never should have lost.[173]

The existence of school district hold harmless liability insurance shields the unions from responsibility to its teachers. Binding arbitration clauses in teachers' contracts regarding issues between the district and the teacher also shield the union. To avoid the time and expense of taking a case to court, both parties agree to let an arbitrator resolve the dispute. (Notice, the union has agreed for you per the contract you're working under.) The arbitrator's decision is final or "binding." Whether you have a contractual grievance (alleged contract violation) or a policy grievance (alleged school board policy violation), they'll be subject to binding arbitration. Binding arbitration can be a useful procedure to keep legal costs low and avoid time in court; however, with unions, it allows them to control the situation and doesn't cost them much. Teachers may be surprised when they learn an arbitrator, not a lawyer, will handle their situation. Both sides are bound by the decision of the arbitrator and each side usually pays fifty percent of the cost. My study of grievance procedures in the ten strongest union states revealed little variation in arbitration clauses and exposed the top-down, national-to-state-to-local expectation that arbitration be used for handling grievances.[174]

Through my research, I'd begun to fear that binding arbitration clauses in teacher contracts precluded them from taking their issues to court. Jerry helped me see that is true and *not* true at the same time. Teachers, as citizens, have constitutional rights that would "prevail over binding arbitration," Jerry explained. Meaning yes, you can take your issue to court if need be. Taking an issue to court and winning, though, are two different matters. Jerry explained it this way: "You sued. You had your day in court, but the court now looks at the binding arbitration agreement that you willingly and knowingly signed or, by extension, accepted through continuing to be employed." Since you've agreed to be bound by your union contract, if you choose to present your case in a court of law, the judge may remind you of your agreement to resolve matters through the contractual grievance procedure. "So, the court could easily look at this and say, 'Since you brought this case to court with full knowledge there was a binding arbitration agreement, you get to pay all the other side's cost and attorneys,'" Jerry said matter-of-factly.

For months, I'd been scraping to peel away the hidden danger behind binding arbitration in teacher contracts. Jerry had just confirmed flaws in the union-touted concept. Binding arbitration favors unions heavily.

1. It exempts unions from paying costly lawyers.
2. It is an avenue through which unions can make or change policy.
3. It traps teachers in what looks like a sweet deal, as though the union is really fighting for them, but actually lets unions off the hook. If teachers weren't contracted into solving issues with binding arbitration, the union may have to pay lawyers to represent teachers in court. As it is, they merely pay fifty percent of the cost of binding arbitration. The district (taxpayer) pays the other half.

The union may not have provided you with a lawyer, may not provide any legal financial assistance, nor be sorry for you should the judge require you pay all the legal fees of both parties. Your option for addressing the violation is confined to the multiple steps of the grievance procedure.

It's troubling that if the need for a lawyer does arise, union members must apply to the union for assistance and wait for approval. Certainly, the union needs the chance to evaluate the situation and give advice on whether it warrants further attention. That's fair. It's a shock to teachers who've relied on their union for legal protection to find accessing and/or receiving it is not a guaranteed process.

Since the NEA dictates the terms and conditions under which legal help will be provided from the national level, all state affiliates have similar legal services plans. Here, I will use the West Virginia Education Association Legal Services Plan as the example.[175] Of course "advocating a position or seeking an outcome which is contrary to WVEA/NEA policy interests" will not be covered, it explains. In asking for legal and financial help, "Failure to observe the procedures established by this plan shall be grounds for refusal of assistance." In other words, make sure you dot your "i's" and cross your "t's" when applying for help. Roughly fifteen pages detail the procedures for union members to get legal assistance, including an appeals section should you initially be denied.

Section two of the legal services plan explains how to file an application, "so that legal funding for representation may be *considered* [emphasis mine]." It makes multiple statements citing how eligibility is determined including that the matter is, "A dispute between the school district . . . [and the teacher applying for assistance]." Nowhere does this meticulous, lengthy document mention legal help if a student or parent accuses an educator of wrongdoing.

I'd like to see the Unified Legal Services Plan list of "ineligible legal services" in reference, which is "updated as necessary by . . . approval of the NEA Executive Committee." Would the committee change the ineligible legal services list mid-crisis, like children changing playground rules mid-game? How would a teacher find out about updates to the ineligible services?

One clear benefit is that as long as you are found innocent, you'll be reimbursed attorney's fees. Well, at least a percentage of the fees. The cost will be shared between you and the union, with the union not paying more than $18,500 for criminal charges defense as stipulated in section four.

It's section five that's most concerning. Whether you receive funding for your legal services is entirely up to the Legal Services Coordinator. Subsection B.2. gives some factors the Legal Services Coordinator will consider before approving your legal funding and assistance:

a. the merits of the dispute concerning which legal services have been requested
b. the importance of the issues involved in the dispute to the welfare of WVEA/NEA or its locals
c. the importance of the dispute to the teaching profession, public education employment, or public education
d. the time limits applicable to the dispute and:
e. the WVEA budget, and the resources necessary to fund the legal services

Which of these concern the immediate needs of the teacher for relief? In view of the union's wealth, should (e) be one contingency? The NEA's 2019 adopted New Business Item Eight reads: "NEA will conduct a study to examine the feasibility of self insuring [sic] the risks covered by the Educators [sic] Employment Liability insurance." The rationale: "In the past six years, NEA's claims have not exceeded $6,000,000. We pay $11,000,000 in premium share. This would save the NEA at least $5,000,000 annually. NEA could quickly build up a substantial fund to cover Educator's Employment Liability."[176]

The NEA, it appears, is spending just *one* million dollars per year on legal expenses and claims for its *three million* educators. Most potential legal issues are being resolved with contractual grievance procedures and/or the arbitration process. Furthermore, despite the primary reason given to teachers for membership being the need for legal protection, such protection is rarely needed after all.

Teachers predominantly believe as Heather, a teacher from Utah, does: "My understanding is [unions] have lawyers that come . . . and they will help you,"[177] and trust the union like Zach, from Colorado, who recently rejoined primarily for the legal representation going into the last third of his career: "Hopefully, I'll never need it, but I know that it's there and it's not going to put a burden on me in my career [having to suddenly pay a lawyer]."[178]

I hope my colleagues don't have to find out the hard way that union-provided legal protection is merely a shimmering mirage.

CHAPTER 20

MEETING SOMEONE BRAVE

A deep understanding of teachers unions had come to light, as when the light of dawn persuades you out of your sleep. There is no resisting; your eyes eventually fly open. So here I was, cross-country road-tripping and feeling the piercing reality on my eyes: *Teachers blindly trust, yet do not understand, their own union.*

As I drove through New Mexico, the same bland sienna terrain punctuated by straggly, deep, dusty green sage brush went on and on and on. The scenery was as unexpected and foreboding as the shock of teachers' misinformed view of their union. The cottony, oppressive gray sky matched my mood. The road to Carlsbad Caverns wound around and around like my thoughts, twisting, and trying to make sense of all the research and conversations with teachers.

I couldn't let my upcoming appointment with a teacher in California hurry me through enjoyment of the travel and scenery. I watched the moon rise over Saguaro National Park on New Year's Eve, the wonder of it nearly matching what I felt about God arranging the upcoming meeting with someone well-known in the media for her stance on teachers' rights. Then the remoteness of the Guadalupe Mountains sharply contrasted the rush of traffic and noise in southern California. I couldn't believe I was going to meet this brave fellow teacher!

My insecurities and loaded thoughts couldn't grasp the magnitude of all that God was bringing together. I double-checked the address and, heart pounding, pulled to the curb. You'd think I was about to parachute from a plane. What little self-confidence I had left me, but faith and determination walked me slowly to the door. *Just a nice little visit to help me gather more insight into the unions, then back to my life routine,* I thought. But God had other plans in mind when Rebecca Friedrichs opened the door that day.

I wanted to meet Rebecca, lead plaintiff of the *Friedrichs vs. California Teachers Association* U.S. Supreme Court case of 2016, to assure her I was in support of and appreciated her efforts, as well as highlight her accomplishments on behalf of teachers in my research. At the same time I wondered, *What if her house is being watched? What if someone sees my car and my license plate and finds out who I am? Then I will be a target of union retribution, too. Should I even be visiting? What will association with this teacher mean for me?* My fears were getting the better of me. "The threat is usually more terrifying than the thing itself," Mr. Wolfe says.[179] I couldn't let the rumors about union treatment of those opposed to them dictate my actions; I moved forward.

Our meeting was no accident, but a God-orchestrated puzzle piece in a master plan. Rebecca and I shared the eyes-wide-open understanding of the teachers unions as well as the desire to see teachers understand whom and what their union was really all about. Rebecca had been in the fight for many years by the time I met her. Her court case began in 2013, but prior to that, she'd been pressing her union for changes as a representative.

"The best result of my experience as a local union leader is that I can say with 100 percent certainty that I had no voice even as a local union leader. The union says it speaks on behalf of all teachers, but really, the union speaks on behalf of itself,"[180] Rebecca explained in an interview with the Free to Teach organization.

The union ignored her pleas for morale-boosting, job-saving pathways. She wearied of having to pay dues to an organization she couldn't trust. So, she and ten other plaintiffs took them to court to end the mandated dues. The court was frozen at a four-four tie upon the death of Justice Antonin Scalia. Rebecca had been praying for and reaching out to teachers across the nation for some time. The court case brought her plight—and that of all public-school teachers—to media attention. She showed me a part of the book she was feverishly working on, *Standing Up to Goliath,* and shared her progress on beginning a nonprofit organization called *For Kids and Country* that would bring teachers around the nation together with resources and support.

"Weren't you afraid of what the union would do to you? Did you fear for your life?" I asked Rebecca, knowing the ruthless rules in the union playbook. She patiently answered me, even though she'd been asked a thousand times. I was stunned at first when she explained that the more she spoke out, the less likely the union was to harm her. Harming her would prove Rebecca right.

Maybe I can speak up, too. A little fire sparked in my belly. I felt exhilarated to have met this brave soul who also loved Jesus. We were teachers, we were now friends, and we were sisters in Christ. The weight of knowledge and ideas in my head was heavy, though. I had so much to put down on paper! I was aching to pour out explanations regarding all I was learning about teachers unions.

At that time, many miles away, another government employee who'd been forced to pay dues was bringing a case against his union. Mark Janus, a social worker living in Illinois, didn't want his money mandatorily taken and spent on causes he didn't wish to support, either. Rebecca was helping gather supporters around him, who also dared to defy union status quo. After the withering letdown of Rebecca's case—locked forever in a tie—it was energizing to hear the battle was still on.

I committed to pray for Rebecca and her efforts and headed north toward the Oregon coast. My cross-country trip was coming to an end, but I didn't realize God set me up for another leap of faith. I recounted the blessings of the journey and looked forward to what God would do next. I was still afraid to speak out too much against the union because of stories like that of Valerie, who'd endured colleagues refusing to even speak to her while the union campaigned against her husband, who was running for political office. Her son was shamed in front of his class by a union activist teacher. Or other examples I learned about including wrongful firings, intimidation, shunning, and name-calling.

Rebecca's bravery challenged and inspired me. I'd begun a blog, started a Twitter account, and set up a Facebook page to begin sharing what I now knew about unions. Still, I used pseudonyms and separate email accounts. I was scared of what the union might say or do. I was scared of the union representatives with whom I worked. I was afraid it might affect my job or the ability to get hired. Fear still factored into my decisions.

Then, about a month later, Rebecca Friedrichs called. "Would you like to speak at the rally for Mark Janus, in Washington D.C., on the steps of the United States Supreme Court?" Gulp. *Me? You want me to be there?* I was over the moon and deep in my shell all at once. She asked me to share stories about my interactions with the union and why I wanted my freedom of speech and association restored through the cessation of mandatory union dues. All the threads God had been weaving together in my life to prepare for this season of advocacy became unmistakable: my politics-talking family, my school board dad, my early knowledge of teachers unions, Christian leadership training, Jesus-following teachers in magazine articles, feisty and feminine role models, a teaching career, a faith in Christ, the research, the miles, the interviews, the heartache for kids and parents and teachers and our country. "Yes! Of course, I'll participate!" I told her.

For days, I painstakingly worked and reworked my speech. Did I sleep? Did I eat? Did I say thanks to God enough? I didn't know what the other speakers would be saying. I didn't know how many would be there rallying for our side. I had to be ready to stand strong despite any heckling or discouragement that might come. Some days my throat constricted and my pulse quickened with anxiety.

One cloudy winter day when the afternoon sun had poked through, the fear finally left me. All at once, I clearly saw the possible danger, the possible retribution, the possible union attacks as an *honor*. *What an honor*, I thought, *that God looks at me—me!—and sees someone worthy of this task at such a time as this.* If you were to look back in my prayer journals from five years prior, you'd see prayers beseeching God to use me for His glory in a way that would impact my country and its people for good. I wanted to be part of something large and bold and risky for Jesus. And here I was, at just the tip of His answer to those prayers.

The realization that God was honoring me with being part of a team exposing teachers unions for what they were emboldened me and gave me a new perspective on whatever was ahead—God was in it, God was for me, and I need not fear any longer. My prayers took on a new energy and tenacity.

CHAPTER 21

ON THE STEPS OF THE
U.S. SUPREME COURT

My head tilted back, my jaw slack in disbelief. I turned 360s, barely able to take it all in. The United States Capitol, flag waving, the majestic Library of Congress, the Supreme Court—site of the rally for Mark Janus, lead plaintiff in *Janus vs. American Federation of State, County and Municipal Employees (AFSCME)*.[181] It was the morning of February 26, 2018, and I found myself in a place I never imagined I'd be. I was exhilarated, scared, and determined all at once.

With my whole being I would fight for America's continuing freedom, for its students, parents, and teachers. In this case, we were standing up for our right to free speech and free association. In the early morning hours, a long line of people formed at the public entrance of the Supreme Court, hoping to get a chance to go in and hear some of the arguments. The two opposing sides—government unions rallying to keep their power versus teachers and other government employees vying to have their constitutional rights restored—stood in front of the Court building at the bottom of the stairs. Only a few feet separated our ralliers from the opposing ralliers. Each side had podiums, loudspeakers, and music. Signs were waving and speeches went on nonstop.

At one point, the opposing rally sent a man with a bull horn back and forth, shouting expletives at us. The opposition would shove their signs in front of ours, attempting to block the messages. Of course, some opposing us stood among our group and heckled the speakers. Later during my speech, when I paused between sentences, a man kept barking, "Huh?" Meanwhile, inside, lawyers were making their fervent presentations to judges.

As ralliers for worker freedom, we weren't against teachers having a collective voice to protect our interests, as many erroneously say. We happen to be freedom-loving Americans who intend to keep being free. Many public school districts around the country function without collectively bargaining with a union at all. These districts quietly operate, focused on serving students and those closest to the work. They've figured out systems for handling problems, such as an Employee Input Process, and enjoy flexibility in decision-making and true local control of their school districts. Collective bargaining is not required for a community's parents, teachers, and students to access educational quality and working and learning conditions.

However, many teachers appreciate the ability to bargain. A local-only union with voluntary membership is an option that can be a force for good. It allows decisions regarding standards and curriculum to be made by parents and teachers. A union free of state and national affiliation can provide teachers with the representation and independent decision-making that best serves those closest to the work. Furthermore, a local-only union sidesteps political favoritism and soft money donations to special interests unrelated to education. For years, state and national teachers unions had the sweet privilege of taking dues from workers as a condition of employment, regardless of whether the worker was a union member, to fund such interests.

I was at the rally to speak up for liberty, for the constitution, for the students, parents, and teachers of our nation. Here is what I said that day:

> Money talks. Every time you spend, you're putting your money where your mouth is. This dollar says, "I want locally grown food."
>
> This one says, "I preserve National Parks."
>
> And another one says, "I help those in need."
>
> You're exercising your freedom of speech every time you spend.
>
> Thus, it's quite an affront when government unions mandate that you give some of your money to them. Your freedom to spend, and therefore speak, is stripped away. Your dollars get used to say words you never wished to murmur. This happened to Mark Janus, and this happens to me: I am forced to pay teacher union dues. When it became clear some of my required union dollars were used to support abortions and socialist ambitions, I of course

could not—as a follower of Christ and for the sake of life's sanctity and the freedom of this nation—let my money be used in such a manner. How could forced union dues be allowed in our country where we're all endowed by our Creator with unalienable rights? Where, as our Declaration of Independence says, government derives its power from the consent of the governed?

I've been denied the right to vote for representation and contracts. I've given no consent to be governed by the teachers union, but they take my money anyway. Don't Janus and other public workers like me, just as our forefathers claimed in the Declaration of Independence, have the right to alter or abolish destructive policies that are placed on us? And furthermore, when it's clear the object of government unions is to crush worker liberty, is it not the workers' duty and right to throw off such oppression?

I've worked in a right-to-work state, therefore, I've seen a school district function without a teachers union. Teachers, parents and school boards are free to act in the best interest of local stakeholders, and no worker's autonomy is inhibited by solidarity and required union dues. In the mandated unionism state where I've taught, there's tension as state and national teacher union priorities are pitted against local teacher voice and local public interests.

The union constricts local school boards, excludes parent voices, and preempts local teachers from negotiating free of state and national teacher union influence. Local worker choices are violated when misguided unions do harm through dues-subsidized motives. John Locke, in his second treatise of government said, and I paraphrase, "We must consider what state all men are naturally in . . . a state of perfect freedom to order their actions and persons as they think fit . . . But though this be a state of liberty . . . the law of nature obliges every one . . . that being all equal and independent, no one ought to harm another in his life, health, liberty, or possessions, for [we are] all the workmanship of one [all powerful] and infinitely wise Maker."

It's not in solidarity or financing someone else's agenda that we are heard. Rather, we honor Americans throughout history because they applied their God-given rights to act and speak out as individuals, and we also have those rights. We trust the Supreme Court will merely be giving a decision that upholds what we already have in place: a Constitution that protects us when we "put our money where our mouth is." Unions entice with claims of giving you a voice. Be wary if believing you must pay dues to be heard. Your constitution already guarantees you a voice. It's time, public workers; it's time, my fellow teachers, to dissolve union control and embrace worker freedom.

Friends and colleagues made other speeches that day. We all had the same message: regain the *choice* to pay money to a union or not, and thus regain our freedom of speech and association. That week marked a significant time for the gathered educators for yet another reason: California teacher Rebecca Friedrichs launched the nonprofit *For Kids and Country,*[182] a movement to empower teachers through educating them about their rights, encouraging them to lift their voice, and embrace the heroic action of opting out of their unions.

Four months later, on June 27, 2018, the U.S. Supreme Court ruled mandatory extraction of dues from government employees' paychecks violated constitutional first amendment rights of free speech and association. It was a win for teachers and *all* government employees.

CHAPTER 22

JANUS VS. MR. WOLFE

During the *Janus* case, the unions' lawyers had said the union would, "Raise an untold specter of union unrest throughout the country" and "union security is the trade-off for no strikes."[183] Had it been a threat?

When I returned to full-time teaching after my one-year leave of absence, it was the first year of freedom from mandatory union dues. As I watched my coworkers pause at a table the union had set up to fill out a union application, I wanted to cry. We were all gathered at the kickoff event for the new school year. I wanted to run over to the union table and start a brouhaha. *Teachers!* I would say loudly, *ask yourselves why, after all the years in the district, are you having to fill out this form again?* We cannot hold unions to accountability if we are not informed. We need to expect union transparency and integrity—and adherence to law.

The "recommitment" campaigns that happened all over the nation at the time of the Janus case were no accident, but were a disconnect from the real reason unions needed signed applications. No wonder most of my district colleagues plodded through the union signup line at the back-to-school event—they believed they were merely showing solidarity. Now that *Janus* was law, teachers had to confirm their desire to be members by opting *in* to the union. I suspected my colleagues hadn't been given an explanation as to why this had changed. The union spun it as an act of solidarity and way to preserve and protect the right to collectively bargain—when this right was not in danger of being removed anyway.

Many teachers could not make the connection between the Janus decision and the walkouts that followed: West Virginia, Arizona, Colorado, Washington, Los Angeles, Kentucky, Oregon, Oklahoma, Chicago . . . Walkouts became a slick tool for avoiding official strikes—but nonetheless shut multiple school districts down—for reasons which had *nothing* to do with real grievances within the districts, and *everything* to do with Mr. Wolfe showing off power. If we doubt the muscle and reach of the union, we can look to the strikes and walkouts of 2018 and 2019 as proof of how strong and widespread it is . . . and how they make good on threats.

The union had begun an anti-*Janus* campaign months and months before the case was heard. Teachers were encouraged to take some form of public action to show their support of unions. It could be standing on a sidewalk in a union t-shirt, yelling about solidarity. It could be sending a Facebook blast to a group of friends stating your loyalty. Supporting "Red for Ed" was also a means of showing commitment.

Over and over, in all their magazines and media and communications they told teachers *Janus* was about "union busting" and "destroying collective bargaining rights." Former NEA president Lily Eskelsen-Garcia is quoted in a February 26, 2018, article saying that supporters of the *Janus* case are "dead set on eliminating the rights and freedoms of working people to organize, to negotiate collectively."[184] Nothing in the *Janus* case deprived anyone of the right to form and join unions to collectively bargain. Yet the union saturated its members and the public with this erroneous idea. Union member teachers were merely part of a pack, with a leader calling the shots. A leader adept at *misleading*.

Mr. Wolfe, knowing full well the 2016 *Friedrichs vs. CTA* case breezily proved mandatory dues a violation of public workers' constitutional rights, and that *Janus* was likely to rule against them, had instigated the creation of union-backed legislation known as "Friedrichs Fix" laws.[185] With the *Friedrichs* case, and then *Janus* case following, government unions worked to put in place state laws to mitigate the effects.

One new stipulation the union had managed to implement in several states is called maintenance of dues. Teachers who want to exercise their freedom under the *Janus* decision to opt out of their union became trapped into paying dues anyway; opting out was allowed, but dues would still be collected for the duration of the school year. Not only that, but opting out could only be done during certain timeframes determined by the union. This opt-out window could be one week in July, thirty days in September, or two weeks in May. Each state and local union affiliate individually determined these windows, but of course didn't sufficiently inform educators about them, nor maintenance of dues requirements. In effect, wily Mr. Wolfe collected (and is collecting) dues as brave teachers battle in court for rights that *Janus* restored, but the union fouled by adding new rules.

Through other anti-*Janus* legislation, unions managed to secure access to details (in some states) about government employees such as home addresses, phone numbers, and private email addresses. Organizations other than unions who wanted to know teachers' contact information were blocked from acquiring them; however, the union made sure to supply itself with this personal info. This information is disclosed through state databases whether teachers want to share such information or not. If you're not a dues-paying member, you have good reason to want privacy in light of the well-known union bullying.

Keeping new district hires in line would be a priority for Mr. Wolfe. The union made sure—because of *Janus*—to secure legislation requiring *they* be given thirty minutes of time to meet with all employees new to a district. Thirty minutes of "company time" meaning the nonprofit, tax-exempt educators' representation is recruiting on the taxpayers' dime. Unions wanted to thwart any opportunity teachers might have accessing the reality they *do not* have to pay dues to a union. This was part of their plan to take care of their own interests, not that of their members.

A while later at the back-to-school kickoff event, I tried to surreptitiously read the fine print at the bottom of the union form. The *Janus* decision requires unions to make it clear what you are giving up by joining. It requires that you opt *in*—giving clear affirmation that is what you want to do in place of the old, onerous opt-out system I had endured. I doubted the union officers at the table were making any of this clear, and the fine print didn't appear to explain it.

I wasn't sure what the union officers at the back-to-school event understood about the *Janus* case. Previously, they'd not been able to correctly explain what agency fee payer or religious objector options were (these are unnecessary now, because of *Janus*). Why would the union help educators be well-versed in the *Janus* case and what it meant for them? Mr. Wolfe would be sure to keep his pack in line, with omission of "a few details" as necessary.

At no time did the unions dare tell teachers the truth: We now have to explain how joining affects your rights and allow you a choice whether to pay us dues or not, since it has been proven that we've been violating your constitutional free speech and free association rights.

--- CHAPTER 23 ---
BOLDNESS

The significance of the *Janus* case enveloped me. I never in my life had felt God's presence and protection so tangibly around me than the day of the rally speech. He gave me the boldness to stand fearless on the platform. My voice lacked modulation but it was firm, strong, and steady. The success and glory were God's.

It's true, my heart sang! "God's power is made perfect in weakness" and "That is why, for Christ's sake, I delight in weaknesses, in insults, in hardships, in persecutions, in difficulties. For when I am weak, then I am strong."[186]

Now, though, I was back at home in the quiet country, returning to full-time teaching while also trying to educate my colleagues about unions. What if my district union representatives knew about my speech in Washington, D.C.? What if they knew about my writing, exposing their union? What if they come across my blog? I was emboldened by my experience in D.C. and a stronger faith in God. Still, niggling worries crept in. I had to decide: bold or bashful? How much did I really care about my fellow teachers? My students? Either I had to begin to speak up or shrink in cowardliness. I knew what I would choose.

Of course, the familiar stresses of teaching were awaiting my return. The discipline policies the unions promoted were quite evident in the district's decisions. Teachers were melting under the stress of permissive attitudes toward student behavior under the guise of teachers' "cultural incompetence."[187] I now knew too much; it was a burden to know the top-down nature and ins and outs of policies pressuring and undermining teachers. The Common Core curriculum that the unions had said "parents will need time to become familiar with"[188] is atrocious. And I feared the day when comprehensive sexuality education, the concepts of which were originally written—in part—by the National Education Association Health Information Network,[189] would become part of what teachers were held accountable to teach at the elementary level. It was hard *not* to view everything skeptically and, on the other hand, important to view it with a healthy degree of skepticism at the same time.

My desire to educate colleagues about the realities of their unions pushed me to continue writing and speaking out. I kept my blog current and shared copies of *Standing Up to Goliath,* Rebecca Friedrichs's book, with teachers I knew. I fought with a true fear of rejection from colleagues and potentially false accusations from my district should my voice against union status-quo be unveiled.

I had reason to be afraid. In Wisconsin, a teacher who supported Governor Scott Walker's Act 10 lost her job because she agreed with the new law. Act 10 limited the union's scope of bargaining to wages and benefits. The union harassed the teacher with false accusations and intimidation, forcing her to quit. In Chicago, the union threw a teacher out of union membership because rather than join the picket line, he chose to continue working with his students at an afternoon club. In the Midwest, a teacher was forced from her job only because she spoke out against a union-backed program promoting the removal of the terms *boy* and *girl* to refer to students. These situations were occurring more and more frequently.

I had to wrestle with benefits and costs associated with being "that one teacher who isn't in solidarity" but is rocking the boat instead. With God's strength, I'd stood on the steps of the Supreme Court in D.C. He would enable me to stand under any pressure I might now endure.

In January 2019, HB 2643 came before the Oregon state legislature. It was an attempt to assess public-sector employers with a payroll tax in retaliation against the *Janus* decision. The tax monies would be sent to a state agency which would then send it to public-employee unions. Unions were trying to hedge against lost dues money. I drafted an email to the committee working on the bill, urging them to vote against it. I queried, "In what way does adding an extra payroll tax help a school district lower class sizes?" I requested they get to know teachers apart from the cacophony of union overtures and stop union abuse of taxpaying teachers and other public employees.

In February 2019, Oregon teachers were encouraged to join a union-organized rally at the state capitol. I asked my coworkers at my school if they were going. None were. We were informed via a district-wide email sent from the local union there would be a charter bus, so the ride to the rally would be free. I figured the bus was paid for with union dues, so it wasn't really free.

The rally was in support of more education funding and lower class sizes. Funny, that's always what teachers are told the rallies are about, yet in the fifty years teachers have been paying union dues for supposed advocacy, they also tell us it never gets accomplished. When will we accept that unions will never stop insisting there's not enough funding? When will we stop being naïve about what is being funded? If most teachers don't even read their contracts, but rely on what they're told about it, it's a safe bet most don't read the union-backed legislation but trust what they're told about it (if they're told about it).

For the most part, I kept thoughts about that specific rally to myself and later learned only eleven teachers from our district went. What did that say about union participation and buy-in? It corroborated my findings that teachers were disconnected from their union.

When spring break rolled around in March, it was a welcome respite for all educators. I spent the week researching more about unions. If I hadn't researched that week, I don't know when I would've learned about the Oregon teacher walkout in May that had been planned at the national level and dictated to the state. It struck me as odd that no teachers in my district knew about it. When they learned about the walkout, no one mentioned that union officials had been sitting with state congressmen, congresswomen, and the governor for months on a Joint Committee on Student Success, drafting two billion dollars in funding legislation.[190]

Just as with the February capital rally, the May walkout provided a way for conversations about the union to come up in the teachers' lounge. There was dissent. Did the union realize not all its members wanted to walk out? Along with the union district-wide email regarding the walkout came an attachment. It included suggested chants for during the rally: "When our schools are under attack, what do we do? Stand up, fight back!" and "Legislature, legislature, what do you say? The schools our students deserve can't wait!"[191]

The teachers I spoke with were confused as in, *why are we walking out? Why is the union saying schools are under attack? From whom?* And I wondered to myself, *why chant at the very legislators the unions have been partnering with?* The union was working up a frenzy about the Oregon Student Success Act. The Fiscal Impact of Proposed Legislation[192] document for the act denotes the addition of seventy-two positions in the Department of Revenue alone just for administration. Furthermore, another sixty-seven positions would be created at the Department of Education to oversee the administration, monitoring of, and assistance with the use of the Student Success Act's (SSA) grant money. Millions of dollars that could be used to hire teachers would never reach school districts.

Rather than raise the bottom line of all school districts and let them use their discretion to allocate the funds, the state would be determining who receives the grant money and how it is used. Since the union was at the table when the SSA was drafted, they already knew it was not a simple matter of more funding and lower class sizes, but a sophisticated web of channeling money to causes and purposes *they* deemed necessary.[193]

Teachers were not told the details. I'm not sure which is more egregious: the omission in union publications of how the funds would be used, the bloated state government it would perpetuate, or the fact that districts would have to *apply for grants* to fund the addition of staff (not necessarily classroom teachers).

Nevertheless, the union wanted teachers to sacrifice a day of student instruction to show their support for a SSA they knew nearly nothing about. Not for demanding the legislature pass the bill. Not out of fear the bill wouldn't pass; the union knew the SSA would be signed into law. They'd been working closely on it with the governor and legislators for months. The union knew the voters in the state had already rejected a gross-receipts tax bill in the recent past (Measure 97)[194] and that the governor and legislators were ramrodding it through anyway.

So why call out the teacher troops? To put on a power display.

Many teachers feel missing a day of instruction isn't good for kids. What are you supposed to do if you dislike leaving your students, but union leaders (and your colleagues) are pressuring everyone to strike or walkout? How many teachers have the courage that Michael, an elementary teacher in Oregon, had demonstrated years prior to speak up on behalf of what's best for kids?

Michael had told me about a time when a potential strike was coming to his school. "The teachers in our district were having a hissy fit, and they had talked about striking. The union was pushing it, so I went on record that I would not continue to be supporting the union and I would not go on strike because I didn't feel that was the best thing for kids." Michael had appreciated his union's support, but when it went against what he knew to be best for students, he was ready to pull the plug.

As the May walkout date approached, our building representative kept us informed. One day she said the union was soliciting teachers' thoughts and feelings about the walkout to present at a meeting with the superintendent. It was a bargaining year and the union didn't want to disrupt negotiations. There were certain rules about when teachers could strike, so the union was hoping to get the blessing to walk out. If we wanted to contribute comments for the meeting, we could. The walkout would also dovetail with the promise of "union unrest" delivered by the union lawyers during the *Janus vs. AFSCME* court proceedings, another reason for me to speak up. As an act of faith, I typed up a message and emailed it, choosing to be steadfast in my convictions that walkouts and strikes are bad for students.

Within a few days, our building representative was telling us about the bullying she'd endured from the union "because of an email sent from our school that 'tipped the union's hand' "—or in other words, revealed to the district administration that teachers weren't in one hundred percent agreement about walking out. The union officers had treated her poorly, as if she was supposed to keep all the teachers in our building in line with whatever the union wanted to say. I cringed. But, they pompously assumed every teacher agreed with walking out; it seemed I'd disappointed them.

It was made to appear teachers agreed with and wanted the increased funding and new policies included in the Student Success Act, but few knew what it said! At issue is the ability of the union to foment teachers to action, even when the legislation is already in the bag. The union tumult over Oregon's Student Success Act is merely an example of what also happens in other states when unions push for increased taxation to fund insidious goals.

Why steal a child's instructional time? The union needed to display power to its own members; to continue the narrative of victory in numbers and declare "look how we're only successful when in solidarity." To create an experience in which teachers might feel a rush of organizational power. And keep paying dues. And recruit others to pay dues. And feed the reason for organizing: more power![195] Even an illusion of a hard-fought battle and victory will breed loyalty. Therefore, Mr. Wolfe was raging with triumph on walkout day (some districts in the state did walk out)—the ends justified the means.

It will be a few years before Oregon teachers realize class sizes haven't decreased. More K-12 teachers weren't necessarily hired, but services for birth to five-year-olds will have increased, and counselors and social workers will be roaming school hallways. Are these better solutions than paving pathways for healthy nuclear family units? Teachers may never think about going back and reading the Student Success Act and what it really brought about: the state wresting away another slice of local school district control, and with it, diminishing teacher voice.

A bit over a year after the Student Success Act's passage, in the union's plans for the 2021 legislative session, this: "fighting for adequate funding" appeared in the Oregon Education Association *Today's OEA* magazine. If two billion dollars isn't enough, obviously no amount of funding is.[196]

My faith and the courage to do what is right had made me bold enough to risk enduring union mistreatment by sending an anti-walkout email. When they took it out on my coworker, it was a low blow. I knew the union wouldn't acknowledge my reasons against walking out because they were contrary to their goals. So, I hadn't sent my email to just the union. I'd sent it to the superintendent as well. It was the only way a dissenting voice could possibly have been heard. I wasn't alone; a colleague also sent a similar email. Our district didn't walk out.

It appeared solidarity lost to the power of individuals.

CHAPTER 24

OPPORTUNITY TO CHOOSE

Along my road trip, while talking with teachers and during long hours of research, I'd merely taken hesitant steps in trusting God. After experiencing the breakthrough perspective that it was an honor to advocate for students, parents, and teachers, I was ready to dive in. So, when a union-member colleague had called me a "saboteur" for questioning the new contract, the local union officers didn't realize I would not back down. No army running at me would deter me; students mean too much to me, their parents mean too much to me, and my colleagues mean too much to me.

Of course, wanting to see the teacher contract before voting yea or nay was not sabotage. The union wouldn't allow me to vote on the contract since I was a nonmember. But since I was still part of the exclusive bargaining unit and legally bound by the contract, I took the opportunity afforded to me by the district-wide email and spoke my piece. I endured the union bullying from solid footing because God "gave me a firm place to stand."[197] I am prepared to take whatever right action necessary to extract students, parents, and teachers from the grip of an organization that cares nothing for them.

While working in several area school districts, I gained a wide understanding and perspective on how the union-backed policies I'd researched were playing out. I wasn't shocked to see the deep, prolific imprint of the Common Core standards. Teachers no longer questioned the efficacy of the standards and students were left in puddles of frustration, blaming themselves for lack of understanding. Would high-schoolers using their personal devices to search "sexual orientation" for a vocabulary assignment be inadvertently exposed to pornography? I would not go along with curriculum that would sexualize children nor ignore the admonition that it is "[B]etter for [one] to have a large millstone hung around their neck and to be drowned in the depths of the sea [than cause one of these little ones to stumble]."[198] Nor was I surprised to find teachers struggling with the same discipline issues with which I struggled.

One bright, late-winter day on vacation in Colorado, I'd solemnly paced up the hill to the Columbine Memorial. Slowly and painfully, I read each family's message about their lost loved one. The Columbine High School shooting took place over twenty years ago. I exhaled rapidly in disbelief, knowing *this kind of thing is still happening.* In fact, our kids are in more danger than ever.

Max Eden, along with Andrew Pollack, a father of one of the Marjory Stoneman Douglas High School shooting victims in 2018, wrote *Why Meadow Died,* a book detailing the current lenient discipline policies creating dangerous climates in America's schools. Pollack refers to the Parkland, Florida shooting as, "[T]he most avoidable mass murder in American history."[199]

Children are falling through the cracks, victims of policy which emphasizes that "Every effort should be made to constrain teachers from enforcing rules, on theory that students will be further 'traumatized' if they face consequences for their misbehavior."[200] Pollack and Eden revealed this gist of union-backed discipline policies.

In the fall 2016 issue of *Today's OEA,* a union article positively portrays teacher training that includes this idea: "We're trying to support other teachers in being comfortable of letting go of authority" and blithely continues with "instead, letting students have their own authority over their voice and their own sovereignty within the classroom."[201] Of course, we need to treasure and respect students as unique individuals, recognizing and nurturing their strengths and abilities. However, letting them rule and reign over a classroom is a recipe for disaster. Who will teach? Who will learn? Recognition of and respect for authority is not a negative—it's necessary. Students don't thrive when adults refuse to be leaders and role models. We cannot go along with unions' desire to let kids go undisciplined, and in so doing, destroy children's souls.

Seeing public education through a new lens was discouraging. How could I make a difference when bound by the policies and power of union influence? I prepared to find a new position in a different school district. Aside from a brief time substitute teaching, I'd worked steadily in two school districts over my career, so interviewing for jobs wasn't something I'd experienced often.

In one particular interview, there were zero questions about what methodologies I used to teach reading, math, or any other subject for that matter. Questions weren't about my ability to instruct, build character, and manage a well-run classroom. I received questions such as,

- What would you do if a child in your classroom wasn't thriving?
- What is your understanding of ACES (Adverse Childhood Experiences)?
- How do you approach learning for a child who has experienced trauma?
- How would you describe the relationship between equity and rigor?

Those interview questions reveal a profound change in the direction education is headed. No wonder teachers are pulling out their hair. I've run out of fingers to count the number of high-quality teachers I know who've left teaching. They've been bruised, overwhelmed, and broken under an unbearable load of stressors.

Would I ever be in a public school classroom again? How could I return to and be part of a system seemingly headed toward spending more of a school day chasing misbehaving children and sitting in a circle talking about feelings than on character building and academics? Why did it feel as though decision makers in the system couldn't look ahead a few years to how these kids would feel when they realized they had no ability to read, write, and compute? We don't hold kids accountable to doing their schoolwork because we're punitive and racist, as the unions claim: we hold them accountable because it's in their best interest, like brushing their teeth and eating broccoli.

It turns out I didn't take a public school teaching job. In 2020, with students out of school due to extended closures and stay-at-home orders, multiple families were clamoring for help from tutors or teachers. Suddenly, the three rightful stakeholders in a child's education could work together free of the education system's errant path. Students, parents, and teachers had the opportunity to work in a harmonious triangle—the strongest shape of all. Education pods and microschools were born, not just in Oregon, but around the country.

Education pods consist of a group of neighborhood families who come together to provide an educational setting for their children under the care of a teacher they select and hire. Microschools work in much the same way, but a public school or a private company that employs teachers creates a charter to run a formalized education pod. Through these, families became aware that they have choices in how their children are educated. Not only that, but they also learned more about what their students were actually being taught in the traditional public school setting.

The popularity of the idea of school choice, which has been a hot debate since Milton Friedman popularized the idea in the 1980s, skyrocketed in 2020 as traditional public schools failed to implement quality education during the closures, and many refused to open. Parents will continue to seek out and demand alternatives to traditional public education as a result of what was revealed during that time.

It is in the public's best interest to structure the use of tax dollars for education in a way that gives all families equal opportunity to access the best educational setting for their children. In states such as Florida and Arizona, parents are able to use vouchers, tax credits, and education savings accounts to choose a school setting appropriate for their kids. Will an expansion of these ideas to other states disrupt the status quo of traditional public education? Yes, and I welcome it.

Mr. Wolfe doesn't like school choice—his power is derived from the *compulsory* requirement of *traditional public schooling*. Fewer students in public schools means displaced teachers, which means fewer dollars in Mr. Wolfe's pocket and loss of control. Remember, the union doesn't really care about kids or teachers—the union cares about power. The NEA has introduced a piece of federal legislation called The Full-Service Community School Expansion Act of 2020.[202] It's a demonstration of their latest power-seeking mission. No one is advocating for children to go unfed, unbathed, or unsheltered, but it is the *union* pushing the idea children be provided for by government community schools rather than their own parents. School choice is a powerful tool *for parents* to be in control of their child's schooling. It is parents to whom children belong, and it is parents who have the right and responsibility to care for them. Yet in a typical power move, unions have manipulated teachers and society to blame parents and look to schools to fill in the gaps they were never meant to fill.

When the door of opportunity to work directly with students and parents opened to me, I took it. I started a company and began offering academic coaching through education pods and one-on-one sessions. I could bring about change to our education system by meeting the educational needs of families, thereby demonstrating firsthand the beauty of a triangle of vested stakeholders focused on what is best for the student. My teaching position is nontraditional in the sense we are not meeting in a school building, but I *am* teaching and students *are* learning.

Parents are now savvy to the choices available to them, while the union stands by spewing fabrications about the supposed "dangers" of educating children apart from a government-run institution. Many top-notch teachers who left traditional public schools and got hired by families to run education pods want to continue living the dream of working within the stakeholder triangle: student, parent, and teacher. Many got a taste of free-market schooling. Yes, there will be difficulties as the nation transitions to more of a free-market model of education, but ultimately students, parents and teachers will come out on top. Let the competition begin. For once, it'll be a race to see who can offer the highest quality instruction for all students, not a lone hungry wolf eager to control the pack.

CHAPTER 25

A NEW PARADIGM

Teachers say they're always pressed for time. "There have always been way more things here at school that take up my time," said Nancy, a talented elementary teacher in Oregon when explaining why she's never been a local teachers union officer.[203] All teachers can heartily relate to that. I am truly amazed at local union officers who manage to juggle their school responsibilities with union responsibilities. No change in state and national union status quo will take place, however, without teachers investing some time in understanding their own union.

Teachers of faith can profoundly impact the direction of public education by becoming informed and taking action in full assurance that no matter what, God will be there. I have a newfound, unshakeable faith that's been formed as a result of taking action. I took a step by refusing union membership. I took a step when I chose to research the policies impacting my profession. I took a step by leaving my job for a year without pay. I drove in faith of God's protection as I crossed the nation in my car. I took a step in every nervous interview with a teacher. Each time, my foot landed on solid rock, the palm of God's hand, and He carried me the distance.

I'm called to live into my identity in Christ, to put on the armor of God, to fight the good fight of the faith—knowing it is only possible with a connection to the ultimate power source: the one true, living God.[204] It is with this faith I'm able to denounce the current state and national unions. I choose to trust in God and I thank Him for the honor of being appointed the job of *teacher.*

If we all spend one hour—*one hour*—during each of our three-day weekends, holidays, and summer breaks to research the unions, we'd break the cycle of being uninformed. (See the list of resources at the end of this book in the Appendix.) Being better informed will enhance teacher professionalism and show a deeper desire to invest in and protect our students.

After some studying, we can talk with union representatives and find out what "researched" programs and curriculums are being planned at the federal, state, and local level for classroom implementation. Let's ask questions to learn what union representatives understand to be true about the union, and ask for resources such as financial audits showing use of dues, latest political and campaign spending, and current and past union-supported legislation. This is not for the purpose of agreeing or disagreeing, getting into arguments, or causing strife—but to *understand.* If we understand the organization we are supporting, then we'll be able to make wise decisions about whether to continue support.

We can ask trusted colleagues to take this journey with us, seeking out information and understanding together. Let's explore the possibility of having a different exclusive bargainer. Let's explore having *no* exclusive bargainer, but the ability of each teacher to choose whom they wish to represent them. Although the NEA and AFT, along with their state affiliates, have dominated for years that doesn't mean they get to continue. What improvements might come if our dues stayed local and our local union representatives were no longer beholden to the directives of state and national unions? How would that improve our ability to be heard? We need to start having conversations with other teachers and staff in our building and read our state's public employee bargaining agreement laws.

Lindsey, a California teacher, reacted exuberantly when I explained that she could pay less in dues, still bargain, and have legal protection. "Yeah! Then I'd have more money in my pocket. I would get to keep my hard-earned money."[205] Very few teachers *didn't* like that idea. With a local-only union, it's possible.

In my school district, 2019 was a bargaining year. That's when I decided it was high time I observe a few negotiation sessions. I've since learned that what I experienced is common: not *one* school board member was present. It's true that all school board members cannot be present because that would create a quorum and make decision-making during bargaining subject to different rules. But to have *zero* of the community's elected school board members attend made me wonder how the parents and other taxpayers in the district were being represented. The teachers were represented by a chosen union-member bargaining team committee. The school district was represented by a selection of school district employees: principals, a human resources director, and a district administrator, to name a few. Most likely, all of these district employees were once teachers union members themselves.

I investigated a bit further and learned that four of the seven school board members at that time had connections to the teachers union in some way. Either they were formerly union-member teachers themselves or currently in a teachers union. Only one had a child attending in the school district at that time. We would do well to spend one of our hours becoming more informed about unions and our school boards and what happens at the bargaining table. Who appears to have the power in negotiations in our school districts? Are parents being given a voice? Is the community being represented fairly when none of the people they elected are included in the negotiations?

Mr. Wolfe is hard at work during negotiations, stealthily structuring a "new education system"[206] that pulls wee babes from their mothers and fathers and promises to feed them, entertain them, "educate" them and (somehow) meet their emotional needs. Collective bargaining is one tool of choice, and he's on all sides of the negotiating table.

If we teachers truly wish to be empowered and have a voice in the education system, we must take the time to study and become well-read about public employee bargaining laws and negotiations, current and past legislation affecting our jobs, and the unions that claim to represent us. We have a *choice* to determine who represents us, how much yearly dues are, and how dues are spent. We also may find we don't need to collectively bargain; there are other options.

Sometimes it only takes one person speaking out to loosen the union hold. Frank, a former Kansas public school teacher and retired Colorado community college professor, felt relieved after dismissing the NEA from his workplace after discovering "what they were really doing."[207]

At the beginning of his career, Frank was an NEA member in Kansas. Then he taught in Colorado at a community college. "I became fairly active. I was a treasurer for our local NEA. Then I became disillusioned, and I dropped out." I was thirsty to know why.

"I think in reality, it wasn't really an insurance policy; there wasn't actually anything in writing. It was all word of mouth," shared Frank in regard to union-provided legal help. He continued, "They [NEA] weren't bound legally. They were making political contributions to candidates they thought were most favorable to education. I was often opposed to their choices. When I looked more closely, they were primarily making contributions to [one party's] candidates, then I saw it as very partisan. No [one from the other political party] received contributions." This confirmed the research of Terry Moe, author of *Special Interest,* and my own knowledge of union spending as well.[208]

"The other thing was that they were campaigning against issues that had nothing to do with education," Frank went on. "For example, they were in favor of gun control. Of course, in Colorado many of us are hunters, so that was a big issue." Frank began having conversations with his colleagues about what was going on with the NEA. "I began to inform my friends that this was happening in the NEA. Within three years, we had the word spread around and the NEA organization at my community college collapsed. We didn't join the NEA anymore."

Greg, a teacher in Washington, shared about his district going through the decertification process and becoming an independent, local-only union: "To decertify is not a difficult process, but one in which the steps must be followed closely."[209] Teachers in these independent unions retain collective bargaining rights, have superior legal protection, and pay substantially less in dues. They have autonomy in decision making and can fight for specific teacher-centered, student-centered, and community-oriented needs. They're focused on local teachers, parents, and community because state and national union affiliates are no longer dictating the talking points and contract stipulations.

Frank and Greg are brave teachers who bucked the union status quo. Others have done the same. In 2017 in Las Vegas, Nevada, the Clark County Education Association disaffiliated with its state and national unions.[210] In 2015, the Memphis-Shelby County Education Association seceded from the Tennessee Education Association and the NEA.[211]

At least three Ohio school districts have disaffiliated with their state and national teachers unions over the last ten years.[212]

Additionally, several nonprofit organizations are working to empower teachers. California Teachers' Empowerment Network (CTEN) is one example of such an organization. It was started by Larry Sand, a retired California teacher, and has a wealth of resources helpful for teachers in all states.[213] Another example is the nonprofit Teacher Freedom. Teacher Freedom works tirelessly to provide information for teachers who want to understand what the *Janus vs. AFSCME* decision means for them.[214] And of course, For Kids and Country is a leader in the charge to educate teachers.[215]

We must advocate for the students we love, championing the harmony of parents, teachers, and students working together free of outside pressure and demands. I know we love our students and work hard for them every day. Let's free ourselves of the wolf hounding us. We need to bring policy and decision making where it belongs. Out of a love for students, respect for parents, and honor for teachers, let's fight for an America with educational choice, autonomy, and freedom.

The insidious designer of our current public education system can no longer hide in plain sight. Mr. Wolfe has been given due process, and it's time to revoke his tenure.

The issues in public education are, at root, moral ones. Let's do what is right, live by and teach truths and absolutes, and discard a system run by an ends-justifies-the-means dominance partnered with whatever "ethics" happen to be convenient.

One by one, teachers are becoming more informed and choosing to stand up to ubiquitous union power. If these educators can take brave steps for the sake of students and teachers, so can we. Teachers who place their faith in the one, true, almighty God can trust in the Lord with all their heart, and step into this battle for the love of our students—despite the powerful union forces.

We were set apart to be teachers for such a time as this.

ACKNOWLEDGMENTS

N o one writes a book without help from others. I'm grateful to all the educators who gave their time and insight. I'm also thankful for the many, many friends who cheerfully stepped up as book readers and reviewers through all the fits and starts. Your feedback and constructive guidance made the book more than I could've made it alone. I'm not sure how to express my enduring appreciation. To my proofreader, Tia Johnson, thank you. To my developmental editor, Andrea Converse, thank you; you're the one who showed me how to put the puzzle together. You also sprinkled encouragement throughout your notes—cold water in the desert crossing that is a book's final stages. To my copy editor and designer, Melissa Tenpas—who patiently walked this new author through the roller coaster ride of edits, revisions, cover and layout. The final package is proof of her expertise. I appreciate her standard of excellence. To my mom, who supplied meals and warm cookies while I wrote. To dad, a model of love for God, family and this country. And to all those praying for me and the success of this adventure. And to the One who is the ultimate and final Authority, in the words of an old hymn . . . the voices of a million angels could not express my gratitude.

APPENDIX

BOOKS

Standing Up to Goliath
Rebecca Friedrichs

Why Meadow Died
Andrew Pollack and Max Eden

Understanding the Teacher Union Contract
Myron Lieberman

The War Against Hope
Rod Paige

Why Our Children Can't Read And What We Can Do About It
Diane McGuinness

Special Interest
Terry Moe

Push Has Come to Shove
Dr. Steve Perry

The Future of Our Schools
Lois Weiner

Being There
Erica Komisar, LCSW

ONLINE RESOURCES

For Kids and Country
https://forkidsandcountry.org

Teacher Freedom
https://teacherfreedom.org

California Teachers Empowerment Network
www.ctenhome.org

Family Watch International
familywatch.org

Stop Comprehensive Sexuality Education
www.comprehensivesexualityeducation.org

Kelsey Coalition
www.kelseycoalition.org

Family Policy Alliance
familypolicyalliance.com

National Education Association
www.nea.org

American Federation of Teachers
https://www.aft.org

My Fellow Teachers
www.myfellowteachers.wordpress.com

ABOUT THE AUTHOR

Kate Bowers has twenty years experience as a K-12 public school teacher in both Colorado and Oregon. She holds a master's degree in curriculum and instruction and is the owner of an educational services company. She writes to her fellow teachers at publiclyschooled.com about a variety of educational topics, including stories about classroom situations, her interactions with teachers during travel across the USA, and current policies, trends, and legislation in the education system. Kate enjoys long road trips and making new friends along the way.

ENDNOTES

1   Aesop's Fables based on the translations of George Tyler Townsend, introduced by Isaac Bashevis Singer. Doubleday 1968 Garden City, New York.

2   www.globalresearch.ca/history-american-public-education-system-historical-timeline-prussian-empire-rockefeller-dynasty/5687403

3   Alinsky, Saul D. *Rules for Radicals.* Vintage Books, 1971.

4   McGuinness, Diane Ph.D. *Why Our Children Can't Read And What We Can Do About It.* Touchstone, 1997.

5   Alinsky, Saul D. *Rules for Radicals.* Vintage Books, 1971.

6   Ibid.

7   Ibid.

8   Ibid.

9   https://www2.ed.gov/about/offices/list/ocr/letters/colleague-201401-title-vi.pdf

10   Ibid.

11   https://ra.nea.org/wp-content/uploads/2016/05/NEA_Policy_Statment_on_Discipline_and_the_School_to_Prison_Pipeline_2016.pdf

12   HOLY BIBLE, NEW INTERNATIONAL VERSION NIV Copyright 1973, 1978, 1984, 2011 by Biblica, Inc. All rights reserved worldwide. James 2:1

13   HOLY BIBLE, NEW INTERNATIONAL VERSION NIV Copyright 1973, 1978, 1984, 2011 by Biblica, Inc. all rights reserved worldwide. 1 Corinthians 13:1

14   Alinsky, Saul D. *Rules for Radicals.* Vintage Books, 1971.

15   HOLY BIBLE, NEW INTERNATIONAL VERSION NIV Copyright 1973, 1978, 1984, 2011 by Biblica, Inc. All rights reserved worldwide. 2 Corinthians 12:10

16   www.congress.gov/bill/107th-congress/house-bill/1/text

17   Alinsky, Saul D. *Rules for Radicals.* Vintage Books, 1971.

18   Paige, Rod. *The War Against Hope.* Thomas Nelson, 2006.

19   Alinsky, Saul D. *Rules for Radicals.* Vintage Books, 1971.

20   www.educationnext.org/accountability-left-behind/

21   www.doe.mass.edu

22   https://obamawhitehouse.archives.gov/issues/educational/k-12/race-to-the-top

23   www.doe.mass.edu

24   *Building the Machine.* Home School Legal Defense Association, 2014.

25   www.doe.mass.edu

26   *Building the Machine.* Home School Legal Defense Association, 2014.

27   Ibid.

28   Ibid.

29   Alinsky, Saul D. *Rules for Radicals.* Vintage Books, 1971.

30   *Building the Machine.* Home School Legal Defense Association, 2014.

31   www.achieve.org/history-achieve

32   www.nga.org/about/

33   https://ccsso.org/about

34   https://files.eric.ed.gov/fulltext/ED569222.pdf

35   https://achievethecore.org/about-us

36   Ibid.

37   Alinsky, Saul D. *Rules for Radicals.* Vintage Books, 1971.

38   www.achieve.org/history-achieve

39   *Building the Machine.* Home School Legal Defense Association, 2014.

40   Ibid.

41   https://www/aft.org/resolution/common-core-high-standards-foundation-all-school

42   http://educationnext.org/teachers-unions-common-core

43   https://files.eric.ed.gov/fulltext/ED569222.pdf

44   neatoday.org/2011/05/17/here-come-the-common-corestandards-2/

45   http://educationnext.org/teachers-unions-common-core

46   Ibid.

47   www.ncsl.org

48   https://files.eric.ed.gov/fulltext/ED569222.pdf

49   HOLY BIBLE, NEW INTERNATIONAL VERSION NIV Copyright 1973, 1978, 1984, 2011 by Biblica, Inc. All rights reserved worldwide.

50   Sanders, Julia. "The History of the Smarter Balanced Assessment." *Today's OEA,* Winter 2015, pp.10-11.

51   http://educationnext.org/teachers-unions-common-core

52   Ibid.

53   HOLY BIBLE, NEW INTERNATIONAL VERSION NIV Copyright 1973, 1978, 1984, 2011 by Biblica, Inc. All rights reserved worldwide. Mark 4:40

54   www.oregon.gov/ode/educator-resources/standards/health/Documents/2016ORHEStandardstable.pdf

55   https://legninfo.legislature.ca.gov/faces/billNavClient.xhtml?bill_id=201520160AB329; https://ccis.org/wp-app/wp-content/uploads/2018/11/Health-Requirements-/Legislation-AB-329.pdf

56   www.oregon.gov/ode/educator-resources/standards/health/Documents/2016ORHEStandardstable.pdf

57   www.plannedparenthood.org/learn/for-educators; https://familypolicyalliance.com/wp-content/uploads/2020/12/Back-To-School-For-Parents_Edition1.pdf

58   HOLY BIBLE, NEW INTERNATIONAL VERSION NIV Copyright 1973, 1978, 1984, 2011 by Biblica, Inc. All rights reserved worldwide. Romans 12:10

59   Ibid. Genesis 1:27

60   Alinsky, Saul D. *Rules for Radicals.* Vintage Books, 1971.

61   www.oregon.gov/ode/educator-resources/standards/health/Documents/2016ORHEStandardstable.pdf

62   Oregon Revised Statue 339.370; www.oregonlegislature.gov/bills_laws/ors/ors339.html

63   www.comprehensivesexualityeducation.org

64   https://siecus.org/wp-content/uploads/2018/07/National-Sexuality-Education-Standards.pdf

65   https://siecus.org/wp-content/uploads/2020/03/NSES-2020-2.pdf

66   www.oregon.gov/ode/educator-resources/standards/health/Documents/2016ORHEStandardstable.pdf; https://legninfo.legislature.ca.gov/faces/billNavClient.xhtml?bill_id=201520160AB329; https://ccis.org/wp-app/wp-content/uploads/2018/11/Health-Requirements-/Legislation-AB-329.pdf; https://siecus.org/wp-content/uploads/2018/07/National-Sexuality-Education-Standards.pdf

67   https://ra.nea.org/business-item/2019-nbi-047/

68   https://siecus.org/wp-content/uploads/2018/07/National-Sexuality-Education-Standards.pdf

69   HOLY BIBLE, NEW INTERNATIONAL VERSION NIV Copyright 1973, 1978, 1984, 2011 by Biblica, Inc. All rights reserved worldwide. John 15:13

70   Ibid. Jeremiah 1:5

71   Moe, Terry M. *Special Interest: Teachers Unions and America's Public Schools*. The Brookings Institution, 2011.

72   Nance, Penny Young. *Feisty & Feminine*. Zondervan, 2016.

73   Ibid.

74   HOLY BIBLE, NEW INTERNATIONAL VERSION NIV Copyright 1973, 1978, 1984, 2011 by Biblica, Inc. All rights reserved worldwide. Deuteronomy 31:8

75   www.supremecourt.gov/oral_arguments/argument_transcripts/2015/14-915_e2p3.pdf

76   www.eiaonline.com/NEAStateAffiliateFinances2016-17.pdf

77   Nathan. Personal interview. 24 January 2018.

78   Paige, Rod. *The War Against Hope*. Thomas Nelson, 2006.

79   Alinsky, Saul D. *Rules for Radicals*. Vintage Books, 1971.

80   Friedrichs, Rebecca. *Standing Up to Goliath*. Post Hill Press, 2018.

81   Scott. Personal Interview. 24 August 2017.

82   Ava. Personal Interview. 14 December 2017.

83   Anna. Personal Interview. 24 January 2018.

84   HOLY BIBLE, NEW INTERNATIONAL VERSION NIV Copyright 1973, 1978, 1984, 2011 by Biblica, Inc. All rights reserved worldwide. Isaiah 41:14

85   Dana. Personal Interview. 14 June 2018.

86   Susan. Personal Interviews. 24 August 2017.

87   www.aft.org/about

88   www.nea.org/about-nea

89   Tara. Personal Interview. 24 August 2017.

90   Mary. Personal Interview. 15 January 2018.

91   Ashley. Personal Interview. 26 August 2017.

92   www.nlrb.gov/guidance/key-reference-materials/national-labor-relations-act

93   Nicole. Telephone Interview. 2 October 2017.

94   Hannah. Personal Interview. 24 August 2017.

95   Cindy. Personal Interview. 24 August 2017.

96   Oregon Education Association. *Where Do Your Dollars Go?* Oregon, 2014.

97   Yorkey, Mike. "Not With My Money." *Teachers in Focus*. October 1999, pp. 14-17.

98   Ibid.

99   https://caselaw.findlaw.com/us-supreme-court/475/292.html

100 Alinsky, Saul D. *Rules for Radicals*. Vintage Books, 1971.

101 www.optouttoday.com/how-the-oea-and-affiliates-spend-money

102 Blake. Personal Interview. 12 August 2017.

103 www.ceai.org/2016/08/teachers-are-unknowingly-funding-planned-parenthood/; www.ceai.org/2018/01/teachers-unions-increase-support-for-planned-parenthood

104 HOLY BIBLE, NEW INTERNATIONAL VERSION NIV Copyright 1973, 1978, 1984, 2011 by Biblica, Inc. All rights reserved worldwide. Proverbs 28:1

105 Alinsky, Saul D. *Rules for Radicals*. Vintage Books, 1971.

106 Gloria. Personal Interview. 24 August 2017.

107 Barbara. Personal Interview. 15 August 2017.

108 Goldstein, Dana. *The Teacher Wars*. Doubleday, 2014.

109 www.optouttoday.com/how-the-oea-and-affiliates-spend-money
110 Vaandering, Hanna. "Joining The Fight For Equal Rights." *Today's OEA,* Fall 2014, p. 10.
111 www.unionfacts.com/payeeDetail/National-Education-Association/1685302
112 www.epi.org/about/funder-acknowledgements-and-disclosure-principles
113 www.ceai.org/2016/08/teachers-are-unknowingly-funding-planned-parenthood
114 www.unionfacts.com/payeeDetail/National-Education-Association/1685303
115 Weiner, Lois. *The Future of Our Schools.* Haymarket Books, 2012.
116 www.defendoregon.org
117 Brief for Rebecca Friedrichs and Petitioners as Amicus Curiae, *Friedrichs vs. California Teachers Association,* 578 U.S. 1, United States Supreme Court [2016].
118 www.opensecrets.org/dark-money/basics
119 www.opensecrets.or/527s/527contribs.php
120 Kira. Personal Interview. 25 October 2017.
121 Judy. Personal Interview. 12 August 2017.
122 www.njspotlight.com/stories/17/11/16/njea-spent-5-7m-of-union-dues-on-recent-election
123 Ibid.
124 www.eiaonline.com/2018/01/11/the-one-percent-leaders-of-americas-top-teachers-unions-all-making-more-than-300000-a-year
125 www.eiaonline.com/2018/07/12/nea-budget-cuts-dont-include-executive-salaries
126 Gloria. Personal Interview. 24 August 2017.
127 Larson, C. John, "Working On Behalf Of You." *Today's OEA,* Fall 2014, p.23.
128 www.optouttoday.com/wp-content/uploads/2017/10/2016to17WEAHudson_1.pdf
129 www.the74million.org/article/six-business-moves-the-nea-doesnt-want-you-to-know-about; https://centraloeanea.org/for-members/nea-member-benefits
130 www.optouttoday.com/how-the-oea-and-affiliates-spend-money
131 Uherbelau, Becca, "Week of Action Roundup." *Today's OEA,* Fall 2014, p.34.
132 www.eiaonline.com/2020/01/09/greenfored-nea-and-its-state-affiliates-took-in-1-66-billion-in-2018
133 Heather. Phone Interview. 21 October 2017.
134 Ashley. Personal Interview. 26 August 2017.
135 http://blogs.edweek.org/edweek/campaign-k-12/2016/07/aft_president_essa_teaching_accountability.html
136 Shirer, Priscilla. *The Armor of God.* Lifeway, 2015.
137 Lieberman, Myron. *Understanding the Teacher Union Contract.* Social Philosophy and Policy Foundation and Transaction, 2000.
138 Susan. Personal Interview. 24 August 2017.
139 Michelle. Phone Interview. 15 November 2017.
140 Em. Personal Interview. 20 September 2017.
141 Nancy. Personal Interview. 24 August 2017.
142 Nicole. Phone Interview. 2 October 2017.
143 Gloria. Personal Interview. 24 August 2017.
144 Paige, Rod. *The War Against Hope.* Thomas Nelson, 2006.
145 Moe, Terry M. *Special Interest.* The Brookings Institution, 2011.
146 "Why Would Unions Kill Great Teachers' Bonuses?". Editorial. *Albuquerque Journal,* 9 March 2018, www.abqjournal.com/1143552/why-would-unions-kill-great-teachers-bonuses.html

147 Mary. Personal Interview. 15 January 2018.
148 Gloria. Personal Interview. 24 August 2017.
149 Michael. Personal Interview. 10 February 2018.
150 Alinsky, Saul D. *Rules for Radicals*. Vintage Books, 1971.
151 Paige, Rod. *The War Against Hope*. Thomas Nelson, 2006.
152 Whitmire, Richard. *The Bee Eater*. Jossey-Bass, 2011.
153 Crosby, Brian. *Smart Kids, Bad Schools*. Thomas Dunne Books, 2008.
154 Murphy, Marjorie. *Blackboard Unions*. Cornell University Press, 1990.
155 Lieberman, Myron. *Understanding the Teacher Union Contract*. Social Philosophy and Policy Foundation and Transaction, 2000.
156 www.flra.gov/resources-training/resources/statute-and-regulations/statute/short-history-statute
157 Alinsky, Saul D. *Rules for Radicals*. Vintage Books, 1971.
158 Jim. Personal Interview. 12 February 2018.
159 Alinsky, Saul D. *Rules for Radicals*. Vintage Books, 1971.
160 Ibid.
161 Jerry. Phone Interview. 14 June 2018.
162 Weiner, Lois. *The Future of Our Schools*. Haymarket Books, 2012.
163 www.nctq.org/dmsView/NYC_2009-2018
164 www.utla.net/sites/default/files/UPDATED%202014-2017%20UTLA%20Collective%20Bargaining%20Agreement-Final%20041117.pdf
165 www.ctulocal1.org/wp-content/uploads/2018/08/CTU_Contract_2015-2019.pdf
166 Judy. Personal Interview. 12 August 2017.
167 www.neamb.com/work-life/liability-insurance-for-educators
168 Jerry. Phone Interview. 14 June 2018.
169 www.nea.org/resource-library/educators-employment-liability-program
170 www.neamb.com/work-life/liability-insurance-for-educators
171 Kira. Personal Interview. 25 October 2017.
172 Shelby. Personal Interview. 7 June 2018
173 Joel. Phone Interview. 22 December 2020.
174 https://fordhaminstitute.org/national/research/how-strong-are-us-teacher-unions-state-state-comparison
175 www.wvea.org/content/wvea-legal-services-plan Accessed 2/13/2018.
176 https://ra.nea.org/business-item/2019-nbi-008
177 Heather. Phone Interview. 21 October 2017.
178 Zach. Personal Interview. 5 June 2018.
179 Alinsky, Saul D. *Rules for Radicals*. Vintage Books, 1971.
180 www.freetoteach.org/2015/11/02/meet-the-most-controversial-teacher-in-america
181 www.supremecourt.gov/opinions/17pdf/16-1466_2b3j.pdf
182 https://forkidsandcountry.org
183 www.foxnews.com/opinion/rebecca-friedrichs-teacher-appreciation-week
184 www.nea.org/advocating-for-change/new-from-nea/standing-rights-and-freedoms-working-people-organize
185 www.ciaonline.com/2017/10/26/neas-post-janus-plan-for-teacher-contracts
186 HOLY BIBLE, NEW INTERNATIONAL VERSION NIV Copyright 1973, 1978, 1984, 2011 by Biblica, Inc. All rights reserved worldwide. 2 Corinthians 12:9-10

187 https://ra.nea.org/wp-content/uploads/2016/05/NEA_Policy_Statment_on_ Discipline_and_the_School_to_Prison_Pipeline_2016.pdf
188 www.nea.org/assets/docs/HE/PB30-CommonCoreStandards10.pdf
189 https://siecus.org/wp-content/uploads/2018/07/National-Sexuality-Education-Standards-pdf
190 https://todaysoea.org/articles/game-changing-student-success-act-to-transform-oregons-education-landscape
191 SLEA. Re: May 2019 Walkout. Received 5/3/2019.
192 https://olis.oregonlegislature.gov/liz/2019R1/Downloads/ MeasureAnalysisDocument/49778
193 Ibid.
194 https://taxfoundation.org/oregon-measure-97-everything-you-need-know
195 Alinsky, Saul D. *Rules for Radicals*. Vintage Books, 1971.
196 https://todaysoea.org/articles/education-policy-budgets-on-the-table-when-lawmakers-return-in-21
197 HOLY BIBLE, NEW INTERNATIONAL VERSION NIV Copyright 1973, 1978, 1984, 2011 by Biblica, Inc. All rights reserved worldwide. Psalm 40:2
198 Ibid. Matthew 18:6
199 Pollack, Andrew and Eden, Max. *Why Meadow Died*. Post Hill Press, 2019.
200 Ibid.
201 "Waking the Sleeping Giant." *Today's OEA*. Fall 2016, pp.23-25.
202 www.nea.org/advocating-for-change/new-from-nea/new-federal-bill-promotes-public-schools-community-hubs
203 Nancy. Personal Interview. 24 August 2017.
204 HOLY BIBLE, NEW INTERNATIONAL VERSION NIV Copyright 1973, 1978, 1984, 2011 by Biblica, Inc. All rights reserved worldwide. Ephesians 6
205 Lindsay. Phone Interview. August 2017.
206 https://files.eric.ed.gov/fulltext/ED569222.pdf
207 Frank. Phone Interview. 23 October 2017.
208 Moe, Terry M. *Special Interest*. The Brookings Institution, 2011.
209 Greg. Email Interview. 16 March 2018.
210 www.eiaonline.com/2017/09/29/teacher-hold-em-in-nevada-as-fractious-union-and-its-largest-local-trade-lawsuits/
211 www.federationforchildren.org/state-national-teachers-unions-continue-lose-power
212 www.freedomfoundation.com/labor/local-only-teachers-unions-shown-to-thrive-in-ohio-more-likely-to-follow
213 www.ctenhome.org
214 https://teacherfreedom.org
215 https://forkidsandcountry.org

Made in the USA
Monee, IL
31 December 2022

24160123R00125